WHAT HAS SHE GOT?

WHAT HAS SHE GOT?

Women Who Attract Famous Men—and How They Did It

CYNTHIA S. SMITH

DONALD I. FINE, INC.
NEW YORK

Library of Congress Cataloging-in-Publication Data
Smith, Cynthia S.
What has she got? : women who attract famous men—and how they did it / Cynthia S. Smith.
p.   cm.
ISBN 1-55611-261-0
1. Mate selection—Case studies. 2. Courtship—Case studies. 3. Celebrities—Case studies. I. Title.
HQ801.S65   1991
306.7—dc20   90-56079
                                                                     CIP

Manufactured in the United States of America

10 9 8 7 6 5 4 3 2 1

Designed by Irving Perkins Associates

To my father,
Harry Scharfin.

ACKNOWLEDGMENTS

This is the page that gives the author the chance to knock 'em dead with a long list of names, thereby endowing her book with the impression of intense scholarship and extensive research.

However, almost all the people who consented to interviews would do so only under the cloak of anonymity, as in many cases they have ongoing relationships with the subjects under discussion that they wish to continue. Others were concerned with the current litigious bent of our society. In the old days, people who considered their names impugned would merely cut you dead in ballrooms; now they'll murder you in courtrooms.

Every responsible writer protects her sources and honors a promise of anonymity, so I can only thank all the people who talked to me. They know who they are. The ones who were willing to be quoted are named within these pages, and they too have my gratitude.

It is also usual on this page to indicate indebtedness to the patient person who typed one's manuscript, but as I do my own typing on a word processor, I can only thank IBM and WORDSTAR.

I should like to be able to proclaim gratitude to all those

kind friends and relatives who read each and every page and gave me sage advice and suggestions, but I'm one of those writers who think that free advice from amateurs is worth just what you pay for it, and the only people whose opinions I respect and whose suggestions I will follow are my agent and editor.

This gives me the chance to thank Paul Gitlin, a friend for over thirty years and my agent for somewhat fewer, and Lisa Healy, executive editor at Donald I. Fine, Inc., for their help and encouragement.

CONTENTS

ix

INTRODUCTION

"What has *she* got?" is a question that has a familiar ring to all women. It's the kind of puzzled query that comes to mind when we meet or read about women who seem to be little different from us but who have somewhat mysteriously elevated themselves to high levels of glittering and exciting milieus by marrying a sequence of powerful men.

Most of us live ordinary lives with ordinary men and expect no more. Chances are, finding the right guy to marry wasn't easy, and few of us can boast strings of proposals from wildly eligible men. Yet some women seem to draw commitments from a succession of wealthy, famous, brilliant and powerful men. How do they do it?

The purpose of this book is to find the answer to the question, "What has she got?" I have told the stories of women whose achievements in marriage have been stellar and have tried to analyze the bases of their successes. Is there some common denominator, a crucial element in the characters, styles and behaviors of these women that serves as the magic magnet that draws the rich and famous? Is it instinctual or an acquired talent? Is it a subconscious ability or a conscious skill that can be learned, and if so, how does one go about picking up this specialized education?

Read this book and find out.

CHAPTER I

WHAT MAKES FOR SUCCESS IN THE MM&A (MALE MERGERS & ACQUISITIONS) MARKET

STARTING WITH WHAT is usually the end IS a rather startling way to begin a book, rather like naming the murderer on the first page of a whodunit.

But this is not a mystery story and giving away the solution will not remove the incentive to read on. This is a how-to book you will enjoy and appreciate more when you know in advance which traits and abilities shared by these seemingly different women have contributed to their enormous success in the love-and-marriage arena. You'll read how each of them has used these skills to win the men of her—as well as many other women's—dreams.

Certain qualities began to crop up as I interviewed and researched these marital achievers that made comparisons inevitable. Hearing the same descriptive phrases applied to each of them by friends, husbands, lovers, biographers and sometimes themselves, certain parallels in backgrounds became apparent. There are definite qualifying traits required to make it big in the Male-Mergers-&-Acquisitions market. Some of the women have all of these qualities, others have most of them.

The one striking similarity shared by all of these MM&A experts is their very ordinariness. They have an everyday look about them, the kind of women you pass pushing carts in the supermarket. Not one possesses the kind of looks that would make you stop and turn or the type of obvious intelligence, élan or charisma that would evoke the reaction, "Now there's a special person." There is nothing magnetic or memorable about any of them, not a single quality to mark them as outstanding in any way.

Nothing in their backgrounds gives a hint of the outstanding futures they would have. No predictions of sure success appear next to their yearbook pictures, no prescient neighbors, relatives or teachers claim to have seen signs of predestined glory in their childhoods. They were always ordinary.

Of course, once a woman has made a glamorous liaison, people begin to endow her with features never before apparent. As a child, Alma Mahler was perceived as plain. After she entered into various celebrated relationships and married the famed composer and musician Gustav Mahler, she was suddenly hailed as "the most beautiful woman in Vienna." Such an epithet seems to have stretched the bounds of credibility.

The same is true with Mia Farrow. A waiflike, colorless creature with regular features, she could at best have been described as ethereal and virginal-looking. No sooner had she embarked upon her highly publicized liaison with Frank Sinatra than the newspapers were referring to her as "the beautiful Mia Farrow." Even Wallis Warfield Simpson, a skinny, square-jawed, horse-faced woman, was termed "the chic, elegant, beautiful Mrs. Simpson" by the press. It's as though a decision is made by the media that any woman who could attract such a high flier must have something on the ball, some qualities of beauty that are not conventional or immediately apparent. And since appearance has historically and traditionally been the only measure of a woman's value, they must endow her with beauty to pay tribute to the status of the man who chose her. After all, if a man who could have his pick of women has selected this particular female, he must see something that we do not, and as he is so great and powerful, we must defer to his judgment and assume that she has elements of loveliness that he, in his greater wisdom and experience, has perceived. And so overnight an ordinary woman is transformed into an international beauty. It's sort of like the emperor's clothes, the only difference being there is no little boy around to point out the truth.

Since ordinary is the common trait of all these MM&A experts, it must be concluded that the very absence of glamour and distinction makes them more desirable. But doesn't that go directly against the accepted wisdom handed down by mothers throughout the ages that the prettier the girl, the bigger the catch she will make? Dye your hair, fix your nose, apply the right makeup and get out there and fight for a man. The more attractive you are, the more partners you have at the cotillion and the greater your chances for making a good marriage.

Wrong.

To the powerful, rich and famous man who has been pursued by the most gorgeous women in the world, beauty becomes a nondistinctive commodity. He looks for other traits that hit him in the psyche. The world recognizes his superiority, so he doesn't have the need to flaunt a knockout glamour girl on his arm to prove his worth, nor does he want to deal with the competition of a beauty. The kind of constant ego-stroking that he requires cannot be supplied by a woman who has her own need for adulation.

According to New York psychiatrist Dr. Harold Marcus, "Beautiful women expect to be given TO. As they see it, just giving their beauty is their contribution to the relationship."

"Giving" is the key word here. The "giving balance" determines the success or failure of all relationships. It doesn't matter who gives what, as long as it adds up to 100% and each partner is happy and satisfied with the ratio.

It is difficult for a famous, successful, powerful man to give in a relationship because, as Dr. Marcus explains: "The famous man gives in his field. He has worked hard to get to his position and continues to work hard. It's usually a twenty-four-hours-a-day seven-days-a-week job." He is thus unable, or unwilling, to give at home. In other words, he gave at the office.

High achievers are equipped with ability, talent and tremendous drive; the talent makes them temperamental and the drive makes them egomaniacal. A woman who wishes to please such a man must practice tremendous self-denial and be willing to dedicate herself to fulfilling his needs.

This is where being ordinary is an asset. What woman with a strong ego would be willing to turn herself into a pretzel to accommodate a man? She has to start out with the conviction that she herself has no great value and thus her only possible path to great social heights is the derivative route; she can gain instant status as the consort of a famous or powerful man.

That brings us to the next consideration. Is her ambition powerful enough to make her willing to pay the price? Is her desire sufficiently obsessive to enable her to commit herself to fulfilling the desires of another?

According to Dr. Marcus, she does not see the relationship as a sacrifice because it gives her pleasure to please the man of her choice, and his need of her offers sufficient compensation. She is perfectly happy to sublimate her needs to his and bask in the roseate glow of his appreciation. It involves no self-effacement because her desire to please is so great that doing what he wants *is* what she wants. If he likes tennis, she will take up the game avidly. If he prefers the quiet of home and hearth, she will learn needlepoint and become a gourmet cook. He becomes totally dependent on her care. There is nothing she will not do for his pleasure—including all manner of sexual activity. Any kind of deviant, aberrant behavior he demands will be perfectly acceptable to her because if he likes it, then it can't be bad.

"This kind of woman has no limits short of pain," says Dr. Marcus.

Her importance to him becomes the sole source of her self-satisfaction. Making the great man happy makes her feel worthwhile. Having been chosen as the mate of a famous man entitles her to the respect of the world. It can be argued that this is derivative glory, but in her view this is not a shortcut to the top, it is the only route possible for someone with her qualifications.

As Dr. Marcus points out, this kind of total submergence of ego cannot be faked. She must be constantly aware of his needs. Pretending could not be maintained for long and would eventually result in her feeling frustrated and unhappy. "You have to be really happy in your role or it won't last," says Dr. Marcus.

What contributes to making a woman think so little of herself that she feels she can really only rate as a mate? Here is where Freud comes in. She did not get the love, respect and attention she craved from her father, Dr. Marcus says. Thus she continually searches for a respected man, or men (like daddy) who will respond to her efforts to please (as daddy didn't) and will prize and depend upon her (as daddy didn't).

The Freudian school of psychoanalysis attributes a great deal of behavior to early parent-child relationships. The obsessions that drive us in later life are, in part, attributed to the need for parental approval and love. It has been said that a boy who has his father's approval will grow up to be a secure man with an unshakable ego. A boy who suffers from lack of love and approval from his mother may be driven to achieve fame and fortune in order to compensate for that loss with the admiration of an adoring public. Such a man always wanted mother love, the kind of one-sided emotion that King Solomon depended upon when he made his wise decision about custody of the baby claimed by two women. This is precisely the kind of devotion given by acquirers of famous mates.

Lest you think at this point that being a totally slavish schmatteh is the key to snaring the rich and famous, I must point out another important and more subtle element: the need to appear to be none of the above. If he had wanted just a sex partner and a housekeeper, he would have established charge accounts with a whorehouse and a maid service. What he wants is not only to be served and cherished, but to believe that these ministrations are being performed by a competent, admirable woman of great ability who has chosen, out of sheer love and admiration, to direct her talents toward the estimable goal of making his more important career and life happier and easier. It would add nothing to the self-image of a man with an insatiable ego to have a wimpy woman who is equipped with only the aptitude for servitude. But to have compelled an independent, capable woman to give up her life in favor of the more important job of facilitating his is further proof of his power.

Let's not overlook the importance of celebrity credentials. The first acquisition is the hardest; once a woman has been the beloved of a famous man, she develops derivative personality that makes her more attractive to another famous man. He doesn't have to question her value because it has already been established by the previous owner. Furthermore, he is comfortable with her because she is used to being with the powerful and famous, and she treats him like a person, not an idol. Having lived with a celebrity, she is competent to deal with his special needs and willing to tolerate his egomaniacal behavior. Being totally familiar with the routine, she can slide into his life without missing a beat; he doesn't even have to go through the trouble of breaking her in.

As you read this book, you will note how all the women described are very much aware that the toughest part of upward marriage mobility is snaring the first catch. Once established as a bona fide member of the celebrity circuit, the rest is easy. You are now one of THEM, and the fact that you were Mrs. Rich Guy or Mrs. Famous Man adds cachet to your résumé and makes you even more appealing to the next candidate on your matrimonial agenda. Unlike the real world's measure of worth in which multiple-marriers are looked upon with disapproval based on the assumption that they must be major screwups to have failed so many times, the celebrity marital scale ups your rating with each stellar acquisition and, these days, with each unmarried relationship.

As you read about the backgrounds, biographies and behavior of the women portrayed in this book, and of the men with whom they allied themselves, you will undoubtedly come up with your own answers to the questions, What has SHE got? Could I do it? Do I want to do it? Can it be worth it? These are personal conclusions that you alone can draw.

Mia Farrow at London's Heathrow airport, March 1968, upon her return
from meditating in India with Maharishi Mahesh Yogi.
(AP/World Wide Photo)

---CHAPTER II---

MIA FARROW

The Waif Who Wins
Wondermen

*0 of human character and passion, the one Proteus of fire
and the flood . . . becomes all things,
yet ever remaining himself.*
—Samuel Taylor Coleridge,
Biographia Literaria

"FLOWER CHILD . . . Madonna . . . Muse," reads the
subtitle of a biography of Mia Farrow wherein she is further
characterized as "waiflike and enigmatic." These words convey a person who defies conventional classification, who
seems to have so many facets and personas that it is impossible to apply one nice, comfortable, pigeonholing label. Will
the real Mia Farrow stand up please?

Here is a woman who has been married to Frank Sinatra
and André Previn and unmarried to Woody Allen, three su-
pereminent men who have three things in common: each
one is famous, powerful and highly sought after. How could
this one seemingly ordinary woman who is not drop-dead
gorgeous, voluptuous or brilliant manage to draw all these
distinctively different heavy hitters?

Sinatra is a philistine who has been described as a man
who "thinks with his cojones" and acts with his fists. His idea
of a big evening is eating Italian food and attending a
prizefight or gambling, always accompanied by a small
friendly band of sycophants. André Previn is a refined intel-

9

lectual, internationally acclaimed as a composer and conductor. Woody Allen, one of the film world's most versatile geniuses, is a brilliant introvert who prizes privacy to the point of obsession. How can one woman appeal to such varied individuals?

Perhaps the answer is that Mia Farrow is able to alter her being to become a companionable fit to the needs and desires of her man of the moment.

To quote from her biography: "Mia Farrow has crowded several incredible lifetimes into one. Now forty-one, Mia has had three great and celebrated love affairs with three unique, world-famous men . . . *each relationship was vastly different . . . Over the course of her career, Farrow has made significant transformations.*"[1] (Note: The italics are mine.)

Insights into Mia's chameleonlike quality spring from a view of her background, upbringing and family. Maria de Lourdes Villiers Farrow was born on February 9, 1945, to Maureen O'Sullivan, the beautiful actress who was the famed Jane of the Tarzan movies, and award-winning writer, director and producer John Farrow.

Maureen O'Sullivan is an Irish beauty who never quite achieved the stardom of her contemporaries Katharine Hepburn, Bette Davis and Joan Crawford. Although her career spanned more than forty years and included appearances in important films such as *Anna Karenina*, *The Thin Man* and *Pride and Prejudice*, she usually had a secondary role and only achieved star billing in B movies. Those were the days of the contract stars who signed on with one studio and worked in whatever vehicle the studio deemed suitable. Originally contracted to Twentieth Century-Fox, where she did six films, O'Sullivan did not know that she had been hired as a replacement for Janet Gaynor, who had left the studio in a financial dispute. When Gaynor decided to return, Maureen was cast aside and her contract went unrenewed. Her move to MGM brought her the famous jungle Jane role with which she will be forever associated.

In 1936 she met John Farrow, a handsome Australian writer who had been hired to do one of the Tarzan pictures, and they were married. Farrow was a devout Catholic who wanted a large family. Presaging the pursuits of daughter Mia twenty years later, Maureen devoted herself to fulfilling the needs and demands of her man and instantly became what he expected. She gave up her career and exciting Hollywood life and took on the role of the devoutly Catholic Beverly Hills housewife and mother of a brood that expanded to seven children. With the same kind of total maternal immersion that Mia would exhibit later, Maureen became the archetypical homemaker and wife. President of St. John's Hospital Guild, working diligently for the Church of the Good Shepherd, running a large home and producing a stream of offspring, she performed brilliantly in her new incarnation. To appreciate how remarkable a feat this was, one must remember that, according to the Hollywood mores of the time, bearing babies was a no-no that might ruin the figure or box-office rating, and that family solidity and fidelity were regarded as quaint, if not slightly bizarre.

John Farrow was a man of many strong beliefs and passions: family, religion and women. Apparently his rigid Catholic views did not apply to adultery; he was known not only for his work in films but also for his sexual appetites. A restless, energetic man of probing intellect, he was a complex individual of often conflicting, contradictory behavior and eclectic interests.

Born in Sydney, Australia in 1904, he initially headed for a naval career and served in the merchant marines and later in the U. S. Marines in Latin America. A romantic adventurer, he went to Tahiti to fulfill his creative dreams and turned out his first book, *Laughter Ends*, in 1934. Then he was off to Hollywood, where he began a third career as screenwriter before becoming a director. At some point, Farrow became fascinated with the Roman Catholic church and converted. With the intense single-mindedness that charac-

Woody Allen & Mia Farrow at a Democratic fund-raiser, April 1986, at the Waldorf-Astoria. *(Photo by Robin Platzer Twin Images)*

terized all his involvements, he began to write extensively on the history of the church and produced biographies of St. Ignatius of Loyola, Sir Thomas More and Father Damien, for which he was made a Knight of the Holy Sepulcher by Pope Pius XI.

In 1939, when World War II broke out, he left his wife and first child Michael to serve with the Royal Canadian Navy. Attacking his new role with the usual Farrow ferocity and talent, he quickly rose through the ranks and picked up decorations, including the prestigious Commander of the British Empire. In 1941 he suffered a near-fatal attack of typhus and was sent home to be nursed back to health by the ever-faithful Maureen.

Once he recovered, Paramount Pictures offered Farrow the chance to direct the important film *Wake Island*, for which he later earned an Academy Award nomination. He won the award in 1956 for co-writing the screenplay for *Around the World in Eighty Days*.

During Mia's early years, he was consumed with building his professional career. Mia adored her frequently absent father. She described him as "a marvelous man, a paradox. He was remarkably knowledgeable. And tough, very tough. But he was gentle. He was many people at once, good and bad. He wanted to be the pope, a poet and a Casanova."[2]

She admired her father as the rare individual with an ability to be more than a single being, and it became the theme of her life. As she told *Look* magazine in 1965: "I'm like a kaleidoscope. I see a different person every time I look in the mirror."[3]

Another clue to her future behavior lies in a statement she made in that article about her attitude toward men: "I like both men and women, but I like men more. Maybe that's because men like me more. You can have so much more fun with men, don't you think? I know that I have. Whenever I fall in love it's forever."

With the role model of a mother who transformed herself to gratify a husband with unflagging faithfulness despite his self-centered excursions and activities, and the powerful male figure of a father who spent his life pursuing a series of identities and succeeding in all, it is not surprising that Mia would become the champion male-pleasing chameleon of all time.

Her frequently reported statement about why she became an actress underscores this need to be everybody, anybody but herself: "I discovered that only in drama class could I make people notice me through this marvelous game of pretending, where I don't have to be me."[4]

Mia Farrow's affairs with famous men have been chronicled in the media frequently, but before Sinatra, Previn and Allen there was a relationship with another major talent of worldwide acclaim and stellar status. At the age of seventeen, Mia began a close friendship with the Spanish artist Salvador Dalí. As described in her biography, they met in an elevator and an immediate chemistry developed. She claims to have met him in New York almost every day after that at the King

Cole Room of the St. Regis Hotel to enjoy afternoon tea. When I recounted this story to a woman who has been prominent in the art world for thirty years, she laughed in disbelief.

"I knew the Dalís quite well," she said. "His wife was a very possessive woman, she didn't trust him out of her sight for a minute. It would be incredible to me that Salvador could have gotten away with teatime trysts—EVERY day!"

However exaggerated Mia's recollection of these early events, there is no doubt that she and Dalí developed a friendship that lasted until his death. She has always said that she regarded him as a father figure, but with her convoluted feelings toward her own father, this does not necessarily mean she viewed the relationship as sexual. It was apparent that he didn't: he took the inexperienced convent-trained seventeen-year-old to a Greenwich Village party one evening where, to her surprise, the mode of dress was none. Dalí had to be aware that the guests were not planning to play charades.

Mia said of Dalí: "I believe him. If he says so, it's true. Dalí brought me out. He taught me the world is what you make of it. Who says it has to be four walls, three windows and a rug on the floor? That's called convention—good for the masses and for the order of things—but I don't want it written on my tombstone."[5]

Two years later, when she first met Frank Sinatra, she said, "I liked him instantly. He rings true. He is what he is."[6]

This is one of the secrets of Mia Farrow's tremendous appeal to a man. Whatever he believes, whatever he says is her truth at that moment in time. She becomes instantly mesmerized by him and is transformed into a proselyte. It is not a pose. You cannot fake this kind of intense conviction and be convincing to men who are regularly fawned over by sycophantic schemers. Can you imagine how marvelous she makes a man feel? With her delicate looks and wide innocent blue eyes, she listens eagerly to his views on the world and mankind, becomes absolutely persuaded and joins into his activities as an intelligent, shared convert. For a man, it's better than getting an Oscar or the Pulitzer Prize. He feels positively Christlike.

Mia is so drawn to superachievers, so driven to capture them, that she instinctively transforms herself into the persona they desire. This is an awesome talent, one that cannot be learned or it will be seen through as sham.

This is not to say that Mia Farrow is not predatory and calculating in forming her liaisons. As she told Hedda Hopper: "I want a big career, a big man and a big life. You have to think big—that's the only way to get it. . . . I just couldn't stand being anonymous."

And who was one of the biggest men in America in 1965? Frank Sinatra. He was a world-class celebrity. When you're determined to catch the eye of a dissipated roué who is surrounded by women who dress to expose as much of every erogenous zone as is legally permissible, your presentation better be unique. Mia knew Sinatra was shooting *Von Ryan's Express* on a Twentieth Century-Fox lot. She borrowed a long white diaphanous gown from the wardrobe department and stationed herself in the sunlit doorway of the set so that Ol' Blue Eyes couldn't miss her when he walked by. To Sinatra, the ethereal nineteen-year-old, five feet tall, ninety-eight pounds, with blonde hair streaming down her back surrounded by the aura of sunlight must have looked like a vision off a float from the Feast of San Gennaro.

But it didn't work the first time. Mia may have a delicate frame, but she also has a will of iron. She kept at it day after day, appearing on the set with that same wide-eyed angelic presence, awaiting the opportunity to make her move. At the end of the first week, Mia was standing by as Frank and friends headed for a weekend in Palm Springs in his private jet. As he passed the now-familiar figure, he said, "See ya later," and then mentioned where they were going.

"How come you never invite me to come along?" she

asked. According to Brad Dexter, who was part of the party, Frank did a double take and asked if she really wanted to come along. She went—and the rest is history. General Patton couldn't have planned and executed it better.

The crude barbarian became enchanted with the seemingly naive waif. She was a novelty in his life and, after all his years of debauchery, must have taken him back to his early days of altar-boy innocence in Hoboken, New Jersey. As a gambit, it was a winner. His racy bunch of male friends thought the combo of the fifty-year-old reprobate and the nineteen-year-old hippie, as they viewed her, was just another weirdo fling for their chief, but the women knew better. In Kitty Kelley's book about Sinatra, Edie Goetz, wife of William Goetz, is quoted:

"Mia was a very clever young lady and she knew exactly what she was about and what she wanted . . . she intended to marry Frank."[7]

Mia had once been quoted as saying she did not want to be just one of the Farrows, she wanted to be Someone. If she had any doubt about her choice of Sinatra as her route to instant fame, that was dispelled quickly by the international news coverage attendant upon their relationship. And guess who initially broke the news? Only six weeks after their meeting, Mia was having lunch at a restaurant with Hollywood gossip columnist Sheilah Graham, when who should phone up but Frank. Now how on earth did he know she was there? Mia returned to the table starry-eyed and announced that she was bursting with joy because she had just received a call from someone with whom she was madly in love. Of course, Sheilah had to just pry it out of her. Graham's next national column bore the breathless headline, "Frank Sinatra and Mia Farrow are the maddest, merriest romance of the year."

All media hell broke loose after that, and Mia was suddenly elevated to page-one status. Given Sinatra's wild lifestyle and Mia's virginal look and the fact that she was younger than his children, the newspapers had a field day, as did the comedians.

"I've got Scotch older than Mia Farrow," said Dean Martin.

In July 1966, Frank Sinatra and Mia Farrow were married. She won her prize and her passport out of relative obscurity forever. True, she had been a star of the TV serial *Peyton Place,* but there were dozens like her on the tube. No more— she was now a pet of the paparazzi and would never be just one of a crowd of starlets again.

Like all the women discussed in this book, Mia was a master of self-delusion. Throughout their marriage, she continually avowed her undying adoration for Sinatra. An unnamed friend quoted in the biography of Mia says: "There was never any question as to the depth of Mia's love for her husband. That's why, even though they have been split for over two decades, Mia has never publicly or privately uttered a bad word about him." Knowing Sinatra's reputation for retribution, one wonders if Mia's silence is due to affection or apprehension.

The fact is that the marriage had its bumps, and they were all over Mia's body. Sinatra did not want her to work. His marriage to the love of his life, Ava Gardner, had broken up over her stardom, and he had broken his 1962 engagement to Juliet Prowse because she refused to give up her career, and now he wanted a nice compliant wife who would stay home and fry scungilli. Mia's youth and dedicated adoration undoubtedly led him to think that he could mold her into an Italian Stepford wife. But that was not the future Mia had in mind. When she heard that David Susskind was producing a TV remake of the movie *Johnny Belinda* and was casting the lead that had brought an Oscar to Jane Wyman, Mia asked her agent to seek the part for her. Susskind gave four reasons for refusing: "She can't act, she's too thin, she's Frank Sinatra's wife and with the wife of Frank Sinatra you automatically have trouble, and she has the sex appeal of Spam."[8]

Mia pleaded her case with Susskind and won the part. Susskind may have been fearful of the possible ramifications of Sinatra's disapproval, but he was well aware of the rating points guaranteed by the Sinatra name.

Midway through rehearsals Mia showed up for work with welts all over her body and red gashes on her arms, shoulders and throat as if she had been badly beaten. Susskind suggested she might want to pull out of the show because it was quite obvious that someone had violent objections to her playing the part. She insisted on staying, pointing out that makeup could cover the damage. Susskind said he felt sorry for the poor kid. But the poor kid would not have gotten the prized role if she had not become such a darling of the press via marriage to Sinatra; she was now paying the price of her express ticket to fame.

According to accounts in Kitty Kelley's book, Sinatra's wrath extended to Susskind. The producer was warned that if he ever dared step foot in Las Vegas and Miami—towns Frank considered "his"—it would be the last step he would ever take without the help of crutches.

Then came Mia's big chance, the starring role in *Rosemary's Baby*, destined to be a blockbuster film. The subject was hot, the director was Roman Polanski, and Ira Levin's book had been a major bestseller. The role called for a full-figured woman. Mia weighed in at under 100 pounds, but the producers were looking for a name with box-office draw. Mia got the part. Her star status and future were now assured.

Time to dump Frankie.

Mia Farrow may be the only woman in history who actually used Frank Sinatra—that is, the only living woman. During the filming of *Rosemary's Baby*, he pulled every ploy in the book to get her to give up her career and come home to him and the pasta pot. Finally, he handed down an edict forcing her to opt either for him or the movie. In this case there was never any contest. Sinatra slapped her with divorce papers on the set, but she one-upped him by flying off to Mexico and getting a one-day divorce, thus proclaiming herself the injuring party.

Rather amusing are the many fawning comments made at the time that evinced deep admiration for Mia's integrity and guts for standing up to Sinatra's despotism, taking a position based on deep-felt principles and asserting her independence. There were no heroics or nobility here. Giving up Frank was not a dramatic sacrifice, as he was no longer important to her; he had accomplished his purpose. Now on with the next life.

Now the driven young woman who wanted instant fame and notoriety ceased to exist. Enter Mia the Searcher of a Higher Truth and Spiritual Enrichment. She was now the pilgrim traveling to India to study with the hip guru-to-the-stars, the Maharishi Mahesh Yogi. After a go at the guru, Mia returned to New York, where she transformed her apartment into Early Bangladesh Bordello style, figures of elephants sprinkled liberally about and sitar music on the stereo. Her taste in clothes leaned toward the loose Indian-patterned flower-child frocks that were the uniforms of the spiritual alfalfa-sprout set of the day. Finally, she became disenchanted with all that transcendentalism and came to realize that the Maharishi's real mantra was moola.

End of Persona Two; it was time for the emergence of the next new Mia and her reentry into show biz. High visibility was the watchword in this endeavor, so she started attending the right parties in New York and London to let the right people know that Mia, formerly Mrs. Frank Sinatra and star of the hit movie *Rosemary's Baby*, was back and available. At one of those parties, she ran into an old acquaintance, André Previn.

Previn, married to the famous singer Dory, had composed the music for many Hollywood films and was then conductor of the Houston Symphony Orchestra. He was alone in London visiting his brother, who had brought him to the party. As Previn recalled: "It was absolutely the epitome of a bullshit publicity party. Hundreds of people were milling around pretending undying love to one another, whereas in truth they either loathed each other or hadn't seen each other in twenty years and would knife each other in the back if given an opportunity. . . . I began to feel very hemmed in and I didn't feel like standing around in that room any longer, so I went to breathe some air on the sidewalk. I turned around and there was Mia Farrow."[9]

How could he not remember Mia? The last time he had met her was at a Hollywood party he had attended with Dory, who described the incident in her autobiography *Bog-Trotter*. "[Mia] had to go across a long patio just to meet us. The natural surroundings conspired to enhance the luminous youth. The background was lit by banks of white daisies. . . . Mia's skin was translucent as though she were still wrapped in the gauze of her placenta. The voice had been gently buffed by good schools and privilege. . . . No pig in the parlor she. . . . This was lace-curtain Hollywood. She was second-generation MGM. And the newly famed waif wanted to be our friend."

Mia's opening lines to the Previns were: "Everyone I love loves you both. So I must introduce myself to you."

With that enchanting recollection, when Previn saw her standing on the sidewalk in London, what could be more natural than to ask her out to dinner? Then there was lunch, eventually breakfast . . . and soon a major love affair blossomed that the English gutter press latched onto with glee. He was still married, she was recently divorced from Sinatra —a perfect pair for the gossip mills. Just about that time, Previn was offered the prestigious position of conductor of the London Symphony Orchestra, a major step up from the podium in Texas. The English journalists went ape when his appointment was announced along with the news that André had filed for divorce from Dory and Mia was pregnant with Previn's child. It's just as well that he got the new job in London because the Houston press had been reporting local

displeasure with their maestro's undignified life-style when
he was dating Mia; the new developments would definitely
not sit well with the Southern Baptist Houston Symphony
Board of Directors.

Dory was naturally bitter about the divorce, but as she
writes in *Bog-Trotter*, she later realized that her own constant
bouts of mental illness had contributed heavily to the demise
of her marriage. At the time she wasn't feeling so charitable.
She was living through every wife's nightmare of her husband running off with a younger woman. André was sixteen
years older than Mia, who was now all of twenty-four. And
she was with child, which, in the eyes of the deserted wife,
is the cunning entrapment ploy of predatory nubile
homewreckers. But Dory had her revenge publicly. She
wrote and recorded a song called "Beware of Young Girls"
that became a big international hit and a large embarrassment for Mia, at whom it was obviously directed.

Mia gave birth to twin boys Matthew and Sascha in early
1970. Shortly thereafter, Dory and André's divorce came
through, and Mia became Mrs. André Previn.

Now begins Persona Four, Mia the mother and English
country wife. The Previns settled down in Surrey, a posh
suburb twenty-five miles from London, in a modernized
sixth-century country house amid woods and streams. As
with every Mia, this one fulfilled the part idyllically. Picture
the marvelous domestic serenity of the lovely, delicate
blonde mother seated in front of a roaring fire doing patch-
work quilting with the little ones playing joyfully at her feet.

She took the family on picnics and on long walks through
the woods. Mia was now into motherhood, and as with every
other role she had undertaken, she strove to achieve arche-
typal status. When she married Sinatra, she made statements
about the importance of marriage and the intensity of her
commitment to the institution and how she intended to be
the best possible wife ever. Now that she was the mother of
twins, Mia set off on her family-building career. During her

second pregnancy, she adopted two Vietnamese girls. She reveled in motherhood, made constant statements to the press about the vital importance of home, love and children. So involved was Mia in mass maternity that she obviously failed to pay much attention to the man who was there to play papa to her mama. André began to develop outside activities, and they weren't such things as riding to hounds. His interests were in the hunt, but the prey were women such as attractive music critic Gillian Widdicombe and a British Airways stewardess. The English press had a field day again, but Mia was too busy mothering to evince any concern in André's extracurricular behavior. The obvious instability of the marriage did not seem to present any deterrent to Mia's drive to enlarge her brood, and she adopted yet another child, this time from Korea, bringing it into what had become a virtually fatherless home. Both she and André led busy, dedicated lives; her job title was mother and homemaker, his was conductor and adulterer.

A musician who was a member of the London Symphony Orchestra at that time mentioned that Previn's frequent haggard, distracted appearance at rehearsals caused many leering remarks about how the maestro's young wife seemed to be weakening his baton. From what was learned later of the many interests Previn pursued away from the concert hall, it was a wonder he was able to make it up to the podium at all. Imagine the logistics of being responsible for a wife and six children, a complete symphony orchestra and a string of lovers.

When Mia learned about yet another infidelity with an English beauty named Heather Jayston, she flew off to the Dominican Republic to get her divorce decree. She returned to New York and moved into her mother's Central Park apartment, which she enlarged to accommodate her seven children (she had adopted another Korean child). That she viewed motherhood as another important role to be handled with her usual dedication and intensity was apparent from this statement: "All I have done is cared about being a mother the way other actors have cared about their careers."

In 1980 Mia went to the Manhattan restaurant Elaine's with actor Michael Caine and his wife, and they ran into Woody Allen. He phoned her the next day and asked her out to lunch at Lutèce, André Soltner's superb four-star restaurant. They talked and talked, and haven't stopped yet.

Mia Farrow's relationship with Woody Allen is the perfect consummation of her years of personality changes. It is as though all her experience in being different people was developmental training preparing her to be utilized to the utmost of her value in the hands of a dramatic genius like Woody Allen. With his keenly perceptive eye, he has been able to see the incredible ability of this woman to perform any role perfectly because of her unique talent to actually BE the part at that moment in time. She has been doing it all her life.

When they met, Woody's relationship with Diane Keaton was over. Woody Allen is a genius and a Pygmalion. Obviously not too thrilled with the available supply of women, he prefers to create his own. He had attempted this with Keaton and starred her in a succession of his movies, but she made the mistake of becoming frozen in the role of Annie Hall to the point of becoming an intransigent professional feminist. This role worked with the characters Woody portrays in his films, but in real life he is capable and self-involved, and Keaton's implacability got in the way of their relationship.

Mia is his perfect medium. She can be molded and still retain the core of strength that has made her challenging. She has become the ideal woman for Woody Allen, offering him the human elements he needs without forcing upon him the usual baggage mates bring into a relationship. He wants a companion and lover, but obviously has difficulty with seven-day-a-week, twenty-four-hours-a-day proximity. So they live in separate apartments a park apart. Woody dwells in private solitary splendor attended by a staff in a stunning

penthouse apartment atop a Fifth Avenue building. He combined two apartments to create a strikingly modern layout
complete with such personal touches as a jukebox. Mia lives
on Central Park West with part-time help in a sprawling two-
apartment spread.

Like many older single men, Woody is enchanted and intrigued by other people's parenthood but loathe to undertake the responsibility himself. Mia handled this dilemma by
adopting with him a daughter, Dylan, in 1985 and then bearing their son, Satchel, in 1988, adding their kids to her previously established ménage and giving Woody full visiting and
parental privileges without any of the spitting-up and tan-
trum tsuras inflicted on live-in fathers. As Woody told the
Associated Press at the time of Mia's pregnancy: "We have
no plans to alter our extremely comfortable and viable living
situations. I probably see as much of Mia as any married
person would [see of his spouse]."

There are times when one of the children goes to daddy's
house for a day's visit, and from all reports, it's a pleasant
time for all. In effect, Woody is living the responsibility-free
existence of a divorced father without any of the appurtenant
rancor. He has the pleasures of a loving spouse and family
without having to suffer through the mundane aggravations
of cranky kids, sulky teenagers or battling siblings. It's the
perfect way to parent for Woody Allen, a man who is obsessive about his privacy and need for solitude. Mia, in her new
and best incarnation as Woody's girl, is delighted to make his
life happy.

Woody's work is all-important to him. He is one of the
most prolific film geniuses of the day and is continually working. He has been fortunate enough to have found a woman
who is not only as involved with his work as he, but someone
who is his perfect foil, his ideal tool, the tabula rasa on which
he can fashion any concept he creates. It is not unusual for a
great artist to use his lover as a model: Picasso painted Dora
Maar and Françoise Gilot over and over. A model merely sits

silent and stationary while a painter invests her with his artistry. In filmmaking, the model too must work, and her performance defines the creator's artistry; her contribution is
vital to the outcome. But an actress who has her own
strongly defined persona cannot be molded to the writer/
director's needs. Can you picture Katharine Hepburn playing Broadway babe Tina Vitale in *Broadway Danny Rose*, then
Cecilia the waitress in *The Purple Rose of Cairo*, then a popular
singer in *Radio Days*, and then Hannah in *Hannah and Her
Sisters*?

You see Mia and Woody walking around New York City
together, both dressed in similar schlepp-chic style, he in
chinos or jeans and sports jackets, and she swathed in
ponchos, yards of scarves and carefully coordinated skirts.
Her adoration and admiration of him is plainly visible. A
fellow guest at Judith Crist's annual New Year's party describes how the two of them sit alone on the couch talking
while everyone else in the room is exchanging the usual
stand-up repartee. Their complete interest and enjoyment in
each other is apparent.

To summarize Mia Farrow and answer the question "What
has SHE got?" is simple. She is an extraordinary woman who
can immerse herself totally in whichever role she has selected off the assembly line of life and perform the role to
perfection. It is an awesome and admirable trait. When I
spoke to her mother, Maureen O'Sullivan, and mentioned
that she, after all, was a role model for her daughter, she
swiftly answered, "Maybe she is the role model for me."

When Vincent Canby reviewed Woody Allen's film *Alice*
in the December 25, 1990, *New York Times*, he referred to
"[Allen's] apotheosis of Miss Farrow." He went on to say
that "in this, their eleventh collaboration, Miss Farrow gives
a performance that sums up and then tops all of the performances that have preceded it."

Each performance is a compilation built upon the many
faces of Mia and with each performance her skills of portray-

ing individuality increase. The relationship of Woody Allen and Mia Farrow offers them the most perfect symbiosis imaginable and offers us a masterful collaboration in the art of filmmaking.

References

1. Sam Rubin and Richard Taylor, *Mia Farrow: Flower Child, Madonna, Muse*, New York: St. Martin's Press, 1989, p. 1.
2. *Ibid.*, p. 8.
3. *Look* Magazine, 1965.
4. Rubin and Taylor, *op. cit.*, p. 15.
5. *Ibid.*, p. 26.
6. Kitty Kelley, *His Way: The Unauthorized Biography of Frank Sinatra*, New York: Bantam Books, 1986, p. 344.
7. Kelley, *ibid.*, p. 345.
8. *Ibid.*, p. 369.
9. Martin Bookspan and Ross Yockey, *André Previn: A Biography*, New York: Doubleday & Company, Inc., 1981.

CHAPTER III

MICHELLE TRIOLA
MARVIN (VAN DYKE)

The Woman Who Invented
Palimony

Somewhere the gods have made for you the
woman who understands.
—Everard Jack Appleton,
The Woman Who Understands

I WAS SITTING WATCHING the Carl Reiner Celebrity Tennis
Tournament at La Costa, the California luxury spa resort, and
holding the book *Why Women Shouldn't Marry* in my wed-
ding-ringed hand when I heard a familiar voice say, "I think
that book is too late for you."

I turned and there was Dick Van Dyke, white haired and
attractive. When I told him I had written the book, the pleas-
ant-looking, rather hefty woman sitting next to him joined
our conversation and introduced herself as Dick's wife. He
turned to her and said with a smile: "This is the book for
you, Michelle."

Their relationship seemed to be a fond one, but he seemed
to see her as an independent woman upon whom marriage
imposed certain constraints. After Dick drifted off, Michelle
and I talked, bemoaning the pounds we both wished to
shed. I must say I felt secretly smug because, while I had the
usual annoying ten pounds to drop, she had quite a few
more, which surprised me. What was such a great-looking

27

Michelle Triola Marvin talks to reporters outside courtroom in 1979
"palimony" trial. *(Photo by AP/World Wide Photos)*

Michelle Marvin with Dick Van Dyke at Tiffany's party for the Night of 100 Stars III, May 1990. *(Photo by Robin Platzer Twin Images)*

guy, and a star, yet, doing with this plain, overweight lady? She looked like the classic "first wife," and I figured he was one of those nice, decent, loyal men who loves the little woman even when she isn't. Then she explained that she had had a heart attack within the past year, had given up smoking and put on over forty pounds, and was planning to go on a diet. As we walked together to the spa, the actor Robert Loggia passed, and she called, "Hi, Bob." When he looked at her questioningly, she reminded him, "Michelle, Michelle Van Dyke," and his face broke into a smile of recognition.

By the time we reached the spa, I had spawned a book idea in my head, a diet book chronicling the massive weight-loss program of the wife of Dick Van Dyke. It had the name cachet that could get us on talk shows and into the big bucks. When Michelle took off her terrycloth toga in order to get a massage, I looked at her and thought, "Oh boy, this has got to be some book. I don't know what the 'After' picture will be like, but for sure we'll have a great 'Before' shot." I waited for the right moment and said, "Michelle, if you're planning a diet, how about we make it into a best-seller? Let's write the book together."

I thought she'd jump at the chance. After all, I thought, she's probably been in the background forever, and here I am, giving her the big chance to make it into the spotlight on her own. To my surprise, she said, "I can't."

"Why not?" I asked.

"Because I'm still in litigation from my last book."

I was puzzled. "What book?"

She hesitated for a moment and then said: "I'm not really Mrs. Van Dyke. I'm Michelle Marvin."

My God, the palimony lady. I looked at her in astonishment. This was the sexpot whose lurid love life had been splashed on the front pages of newspapers and in magazines all over the world? This was the infamous woman who had been the chosen beloved of Oscar-winning Lee Marvin? Granted, that case was at least ten years old, but I looked carefully for even a vestige of whatever it was that had drawn her to the attention of Lee Marvin, and now to delightful, charming Dick Van Dyke, but my search went down in defeat. Maybe the body had gone and she had become a stylish stout, but what about sparkling personality, or maybe dancing eyes, or bubbling wit, or even sweet, winning charm? Zilch. *Nada*. She had a pleasing face, but looked like she'd be more at home in the aisle of a supermarket than one at the Dorothy Chandler Pavilion, where they often give out the Oscars. I was nonplussed. All I kept thinking as we talked was: "What has *she* got?"

How on earth did this very ordinary woman attract these knockout guys who, especially in Southern California, have a virtual harem of gorgeous idolizing nymphets and sexy starlets from whom to choose mates? And she didn't just draw their interest for a mere Hollywood quickie, but for a long-term relationship. As I later learned from our talk, Michelle has been living with Dick Van Dyke for eleven years. Her liaison with Lee Marvin had lasted six years. She moved in with Dick right after the trial in 1979, the one that ended with the judge awarding her $104,000 to equal two years of her average working income (she claimed to have made $1,000 a week at the height of her singing career), for "rehabilitative purposes . . . to reeducate herself and learn new employable skills." The judge later added that he gave her the money so she could "return from her status as companion of a motion-picture star to a separate calling . . . an independent but perhaps more prosaic existence." But I guess she didn't need new skills; the old ones seemed to be in excellent working order.

At the time Dick Van Dyke fell in love with her and asked her to become his live-in, she was forty-six years old. In Hollywood, that's a senior citizen. When you consider the competition, one must conclude that Michelle possesses some compelling qualities that may not be readily apparent.

Michelle Triola was born in Chicago in 1933. After finish-

ing high school, she followed the star-struck route of thousands of pretty girls whose talent seems impressive when
placed next to the klutzes at Madame Shirley's local dance
school and headed for Hollywood, where she soon found
out that what flies in Illinois can't even get off the ground in
L.A. She got jobs singing in nightclubs, and traveled the
usual skin-showing dancing circuit of Las Vegas, Reno and
the Playboy Clubs. Meanwhile, Mom and Dad back home
kept pressing Michelle to do what young women of the
1950s were supposed to—get married and settle down. So at
age twenty-seven, Michelle married an actor named Skip
Ward. The marriage lasted less than a year. According to a
New York Times interview she gave years later, Michelle
claimed, "We were both too immature."[1] Continuing her
career, she moved on to Europe, where she sang in nightclubs and earned between $300 and $1,000 a week. Then in
1974 Michelle got a break, a small part as a dancer in the
film *Ship of Fools*, which starred, among others, the actor Lee
Marvin. It turned out to be a role that would change her life.

As she told the *Times* reporter, "Then I met Lee, and my
life was never the same. After a few weeks of dating, he
moved into my apartment. For the next six years, we were
together."

Lee bought a $250,000 beach house in Malibu, that glitzy
stretch of sand where millionaire moviemakers make merry
and where your next-door neighbor is more likely to drop in
to borrow a bottle of booze or a snort of coke than a cup of
sugar. Michelle spent her time decorating their home and
acting as companion, cook, cleaner and confidante for Lee, as
she later claimed in her lawsuit. She also stated that her trying out duties in their household involved not only the
clothes and the dishes, but helping Lee dry out after an alcoholic binge. It seemed like a typical Hollywood marriage
except that matrimonial vows never entered the picture. According to Michelle, Lee promised to support her for life and
told her that a piece of paper didn't mean anything. "What I

have is yours and what you have is mine," he told her, and it must have seemed a good deal to her at the time, since she had bubkis.

The concept of "open marriage" was greeted by the American public as a hot new idea when it was introduced in the sixties, but show-biz folk have always regarded marital fidelity as quaint and consider outside sexual activity a regular part of their fitness programs. Therefore, we can assume that the behavior of a movie bit player named Richard Doughty (as revealed in his sworn testimony at trial) would in no way have impinged on Lee and Michelle's loving relationship. Doughty claimed to have made love to Michelle "just about every day" during the Palau Islands filming of the movie *Hell in the Pacific* (the picture took twenty-five days to shoot). But Michelle was happily at Lee's side when he won an Oscar for his performance in *Cat Ballou*. Somewhere along the way, she even changed her name legally to Michelle Marvin, the name that still appears on her passport.

The less happy part of their life together involved three pregnancies, two ending in abortion and one in miscarriage, and, of course, Lee's legendary alcoholism.

In 1970 Lee decided he wanted out, and went back to his hometown of Woodstock, a village in New York's Catskill Mountains, and married his high school sweetheart, Pamela Feeley. To compensate Michelle for his defection, he agreed to pay her $800 a month for five years, but stopped after one year. He claimed he cut her off because he believed she was the source of a leak to gossip columnists that his marriage was on the rocks. But Lee was dealing with the wrong wronged lady; Michelle was no limp wimp and she went to Marvin Mitchelson, the attorney known for his megabuck wins, and asked him to find a way to get her the promised half of Marvin's earnings during their years together when he accumulated millions of dollars from smash hit movies such as *Cat Ballou* and *The Dirty Dozen*.

Mitchelson, feeling that Michelle's cause was just and possibly considering that the landmark concept of cohabiting couples having the same financial sharing obligations as married couples could open up a veritable bonanza of lucrative litigation for him, agreed to take her case.

Two courts tossed out the case. In 1972 the trial court and the intermediate appellate courts ruled that a woman living with a man to whom she is not married is involved in what is called a "meretricious" relationship—which really means whorelike—and that the state should not enforce contracts made under such immoral circumstances. But Michelle and Mitchelson were a formidable, determined team and they appealed. On December 27, 1976, the California Supreme Court overturned the lower courts with an opinion that reflected judicial recognition of the tremendous change in current life-styles by stating that in the light of so many live-togethers, the meretricious doctrine was no longer valid, and Michelle was indeed entitled to a trial.

By the time the case opened in January 1979, Michelle had become a heroine of the feminist movement. Spectators queued up every day for eleven weeks to watch what became exciting theater. *Newsweek* described it in a full-page story. "She was petite and demure in tasteful blue blazer or pantsuit. He was the aging star, silver-haired, and baggy-eyed, dapper in custom-tailored suits. Her fans gave her roses; his asked for autographs. . . . *Marvin versus Marvin* offered tales of love, and unfaithfulness, abortions and threatened suicides, spicy tidbits about the sexual and financial habits of celebrities—and even some legal issues of consequence. 'It's like a good script,' Lee Marvin observed."[2]

Mitchelson's position was that Michelle had, at Marvin's request, given up a burgeoning career in order to perform all the caretaking functions of a wife. When he abandoned her six years later, she had lost out on critical career-building years and was now a thirty-seven-year-old former singer who hadn't been on a stage for six years, not exactly the kind of credentials to light up the eyes of booking agents. She was reduced to supporting herself by watering plants, typing, and doing odd jobs for friends until she found a $125-a-week job at the William Morris Agency in Beverly Hills. Michelle maintained that she had given Lee the best years of her life, was to all intents and purposes his spouse and thus was not only entitled to the California community-property stipulation of one-half of money earned during their years together, but to alimony.

The conclusion of the case hit the front page of the *New York Times* on April 19, 1979, and was illustrated with twin smiling pictures of the once happy couple, each claiming victory. However, there is no doubt that Lee Marvin won. Judge Arthur Marshall of the Los Angeles Supreme Court denied that Michelle had an explicit or even implied contract with Lee that entitled her to any portion of his property. Judge Marshall, a domestic relations expert, raised doubts about Michelle's credibility and concluded that the relationship was not marriagelike, which was essentially what she had to prove under the developing rules of "palimony." But he threw her a going-away present of the legal equivalent of rehabilitative alimony.

In an April 19 *New York Times* interview, Michelle said she looked forward "to playing tennis and resting before embarking on a new career as a talent agent." Right after the trial, she told an Associated Press reporter that she was "disillusioned with love affairs" and said bitterly, "I think if a man wants to leave a toothbrush in my house, he can bloody well marry me." Either her disillusionment was very short-lived or Dick Van Dyke was very persuasive and appealing, because she moved in with him without benefit of wedlock almost immediately after the trial. In fact, she told me that she was considering this during the trial, but lawyer Mitchelson advised her to wait until after the proceedings were concluded.

The case did not win any significant money for Michelle, as Marvin Mitchelson doesn't come cheap, and the $104,000 she was awarded probably wouldn't cover his annual florist's bill. But she did win legend status and a place in the hearts of all feminists. The ancillary financial opportunities arising from her association with the new word "palimony" should not be taken lightly.

The first step in capitalizing on her new-found fame was embarking on the inevitable book, but the project did not conclude happily, due to differences of opinion between Michelle and the "as told to" writer. There is a promise of a book in the future. Recognition of her name today is universal and instant. Whenever I mentioned Michelle Marvin as one of the subjects of this book, eyes always lit up and the word "palimony" was mentioned. As a result, she does well on the lecture circuit and appears before women's groups and clubs who want to hear and see the famous "palimony lady" in the flesh.

As we talked about the lecturing, Michelle mentioned her annoyance with women who come up after the talk and ask her outright, "What have YOU got that gets these great guys?"

"What do you answer?" I asked, agog with anticipation, as that was the unaskable question going through *my* mind.

She looked properly indignant. "I tell them that I am a very independent person, and I believe 'to thine own self be true.'"

Words to live by, and so refreshing coming from a woman who has built her life on alliances with famous men. What's interesting is that Michelle sincerely believes she is a staunch feminist. She told me how furious she had become at her cardiologist when he came into her hospital room to advise her that she would soon be totally recovered, and using his best Beverly Hills bedside manner, jovially assured her that she could look forward to the resumption of her routine of enjoying full use of her credit cards at all the smart shops. It is the kind of avuncular remark that makes women livid and sends feminists to the ramparts. Michelle told me with great satisfaction that she told him to fuck off.

Perhaps Michelle's self-perception as a feminist is not off the wall. Many of the women in this book expressed similar positions. Women who have made their marks in life via liaisons with important men and have, in effect, lived derivative existences, would seem to be the very antithesis of feminists. However, it is not what you do, but how you feel about it that defines you.

At no point in our conversation did Michelle indicate that she wanted to marry Dick or to live any way but in unwed cohabitation. Yet, although she may do some lecturing and talk about writing a book, in fact her major occupation is companion and homemaker for Dick Van Dyke. From my observation and all reports, she does a fine job. When we discussed arrangements for a later interview, she mentioned that it could not be a specific week because Dick would be working then, and she said with the proprietary pride of the needed woman, "He likes me to be around when he's working," a fact corroborated by his agent.

Yet she does not come off as a submissive spouse whose sole mission in life is devoting herself to the care and feeding of her man. Quite the contrary, she conveys a sense of independence. Is this, then, part of the secret that enables a seemingly ordinary woman to snare an extraordinary famous man? Is it the legerdemain of managing to create the image of a forceful woman so as to give the man the false satisfaction that he has won a difficult-to-get prize, but in actuality catering to his domestic, egotistical and sexual needs? Of course, what you or I might put under the heading of "catering to," Michelle might regard as mere garden-variety cohabiting responsibilities. When we talked about male-female relationships, Michelle mentioned an eighty-two-year-old male friend who had recently left his wife of well over fifty years and was now deliriously happy with a wonderful twenty-eight-year-old woman who "gives him head three times a day." When my involuntarily issued "Yuck!" indicated that I didn't consider that performing oral sex with an octogenarian qualified this young woman for the Admirable Woman's Hall of Fame, Michelle looked surprised. "But if it makes her happy to make him happy, what's wrong with that?"

What, indeed, but before we think of fitting this warm-hearted woman with a halo for her efforts to bring joy into the dwindling life of a very senior citizen, let me add that this fulfilled elderly gentleman is the owner of a huge retail empire and is able to show his gratitude with much more than a thank you and a pat on the tush. Apparently, Michelle's value system for human relations allows no conflict between self-esteem and servility and in her mind the end always justifies the means, if you'll pardon the expression. She may see no contradiction in condoning this sort of behavior and considering herself a feminist, but somehow I just can't see Gloria Steinem in this part.

How could a woman appeal to two men as disparate as Lee Marvin and Dick Van Dyke? One was crude and simple and the other, gentle and soft-spoken. One was a man whose conversation consisted primarily of grunts, eye rolls and shrugs; the other, an articulate charmer who loves Bach and reads Kierkegaard. With one, Michelle lived a bawdy, boisterous life; with the other, a serenely domestic existence. It boggles the mind to comprehend how she has filled the needs of such total opposites. Could it be that Michelle Triola is Everywoman, all things to all men? How else can you explain her appeal to such divergent personalities?

There is one common denominator—alcoholism. Lee Marvin was a dedicated drinker, a man described by Lewis Grossberger in an article in the August 25, 1980, issue of *New York* magazine, as "The ultimate drinking buddy . . .

he doesn't even need a saloon . . . he carries one with him like an aura."[3]

He was a coarse, brutish-looking man described in the article as looking "spectacularly mean and ugly—that great menacing Easter Island face looms over you."[4] The writer alluded to Lee's inability to talk properly, or even remember names: "Entire sentences get lost. Lee launches into a rollicking Hollywood story, but somewhere along the way he has misplaced a fact vital to its comprehension. Or he will come careening up to some key phrase or image and skid to a halt, unable to find the word."[5]

Lee was a natural actor who, if not for World War II, would have been a plumber. After getting out of high school, he became apprenticed to Woodstock's leading plumber. However, the war intervened and while in the service, Lee became interested in acting and began a totally new and unplanned career in theatre and movies. His intimidating demeanor, narrow-eyed killer face and gravelly morning-after voice made him a natural for action movies. He played cops, commandos and cowboys and never seemed complete without a gun. He projected a powerful macho image, every man's dream of the invulnerable tough guy who can handle anything and anybody. But like most people who become alcoholics, he was riddled with feelings of inadequacy. He knew he was not terribly bright or intellectual and was aware that he could never fit in with Hollywood's smart set.

"I was sitting with Jack Lemmon and Johnny Carson," he said in the *New York* interview, "all the smarties, you know, the quick one-liners. Snappy conversation, zing-zing. And you know I don't worry about it because they're not in my league anyway. Or I'm not in theirs."[6]

Insecure, with feelings of inadequacy, Lee Marvin was unhappy being with people he felt were better than he. Brainy people diminished him, gorgeous women disquieted him. He was discomfited by superiority and comfortable only with ordinary folk—like Michelle Triola.

According to Vernon E. Johnson, founder of the Johnson Institute in Minnesota for the treatment of alcoholism, in his book *I'll Quit Tomorrow*, alcoholics are filled with despair at their worthlessness and tremendous guilt for what they perceive as their flawed, inadequate behavior. "In searching for common denominators," he writes, "we have observed that the alcoholic is likely to be an achiever."[7] A person who has reached a position the world regards as successful but who feels he is unqualified for the role derides himself for being an impostor who risks being exposed at any time and often turns to alcohol to escape the fears. This is the sort of demon that bedeviled Lee Marvin and also Dick Van Dyke.

It seems incredible that a superbly talented, successful and wealthy man such as Dick Van Dyke would suffer from a sense of inadequacy. But as every psychotherapist will tell you, facts have nothing to do with feelings.

"A guy who feels good and then tries to find out why he feels good may soon find he has no reason for it and end up miserable,"[8] said Van Dyke in an interview with Jack Leay for the *New York Times Magazine* published November 18, 1962. It tells of a man who is afraid to probe his feelings and explains the sort of fear that can be temporarily assuaged by alcohol. As a recovered alcoholic, Van Dyke explained his past drinking in a January 1982 article in *The Saturday Evening Post*. "I was neurotically insecure. Now I take a more serene attitude toward everything. I think anyone does as they get older. When you're young, there's the fear of not working. You feel competitive with your peers . . . talent is such an ephemeral thing. What is it? . . . I can take failure now."[9]

Dick Van Dyke was born in 1925 and brought up in a conventional Midwestern household in Danville, Illinois. In 1948, he married his childhood sweetheart on the "Bride and Groom" radio show, where the reward for this nuptial exhibitionism was a pile of gifts, cash and goodies. After the birth of his first two children (he has four), he broke into television and was soon a highly successful daytime performer, filling in for the vacationing Garry Moore, anchoring *The Morning Show* and hosting around the dial. In 1960, he won the starring role on Broadway in *Bye Bye Birdie*, which he repeated in the movie. In 1962, he was tapped by Carl Reiner to star in his new series and the rest is TV history. Through all these career-building years, Dick taught Sunday school and was always described as a family man who spent a lot of time with his children, a factor that is always regarded as noteworthy in Hollywood, where parenting is regarded as a puzzling role for which there are no models. This man sounds successful and fulfilled; he should have been utterly devoid of self-doubts. Yet he turned to alcohol.

According to Vernon Johnson, alcoholics actually know little of themselves and are loaded with repressed self-hatred. A man with this minimal sense of self-worth would not feel deserving of a gorgeous knockout girlfriend and would be more comfortable with an ordinary woman like Michelle Triola.

It is interesting to note that both Lee Marvin and Dick Van Dyke married their childhood sweethearts—nice, plain girls —Dick early and Lee later on. (The Van Dykes divorced in 1984.) People gravitate to whatever makes them comfortable, wherever they feel they fit in. I have a friend who has always lived in seedy houses. Even though she is able to afford the luxurious homes shown her over the years by a succession of puzzled real estate agents, she inevitably buys the slightly grungy places to which she is drawn by a sense of familiarity. She walks through the drop-dead decors with marble baths and Jacuzzis, but somehow cannot see herself living there. It may be nice to visit, but it's not home.

To insecure men such as Lee Marvin and Dick Van Dyke, Michelle Triola is a woman with whom they BELONG. They feel at home, relaxed and contented. She is the perfect person for their imperfect world. She is nice-looking, but not overwhelmingly so. She is intelligent, but not overwhelmingly so. She is a companion, but never a threat. And she is an experienced caretaker of alcoholics and thus able to handle any concomitant sexual or personal problem that arises. She conveys a sense of being her own person, so men never need fear being burdened with a cloying dependent, which can be a real drag to such men.

What does Michelle Triola Marvin have that attracted two famous Hollywood men? She was there when they were looking for an ordinary woman in a tinsel town crawling with extravagantly extraordinary people.

References

1. *New York Times*, April 18, 1979.
2. "An Unmarried Woman," J. K. Footlick and M. Kasindorf, *Newsweek*, April 30, 1979.
3. "The Ultimate Drinking Buddy," Lewis Grossberger, *New York*, August 25, 1980, p. 48.
4. *Ibid.*
5. *Ibid.*
6. *Ibid.*
7. Vernon E. Johnson, *I'll Quit Tomorrow*, New York: Harper & Row, 1980.
8. *New York Times Magazine*, November 18, 1962.
9. "The Serious Side of Dick Van Dyke," Sally Saunders, *Saturday Evening Post*, January-February 1982, p. 64.

CHAPTER IV

FRANÇOISE GILOT

The Woman of Two Titans
(Picasso and Salk)

It's a sort of bloom on a woman. If you have [charm] you
don't need to have anything else, and if you don't have it,
it doesn't much matter what else you have.
—J. M. Barry,
What Every Woman Knows

FRANÇOISE GILOT has been the choice of two of the greatest men of the twentieth century, each of whom literally changed the world. Pablo Picasso gave us new insights into life through art, and Jonas Salk gave actual life to millions of children who might have died from polio if not for his great vaccine discovery. Françoise Gilot lived with Picasso for ten years and bore two of his children, Paloma and Claude. For the past twenty years, she has been the wife of Dr. Jonas Salk and divides her time between their home in San Diego near the famous Salk Institute and her apartments in New York City and Paris.

Two geniuses, yet no two men could be more different. Pablo Picasso was born to Catholic parents in Málaga, Spain, and spent his entire creative life in France. He was explosive, moody, abusive, lusty and, although he had little formal education, was highly intelligent and political. Jonas Salk was born in the United States to Lithuanian Jewish immigrant parents. He is brilliant, highly educated, cool, competent, elegant and philosophical. What is it about Françoise Gilot

43

Françoise Gilot standing alongside her paintings at exhibit in Sarasota, Florida gallery, October 1975. *(AP/World Wide Photos)*

that made two such dissimilar men commit themselves to her and desire to have her devote herself solely to them?

When I saw her standing in the open doorway of her New York apartment, my first reaction was shock at her ordinariness followed by the sudden realization of the self-confidence of a sixty-eight-year-old woman who can wear slacks and a sweater, absolutely no makeup, glasses perched on her nose, and greet me with the assurance and poise of a queen.

Françoise Gilot is a woman who does not place great store in conventionally female surface artifices but rather relies on the great force of her charm, intelligence and vivacity to create an impact. I looked at her in the bright cruel daylight and saw the wonderful cheekbone structure, elegantly shaped nose and long oval face that have been made familiar by the Picasso portraits.

In her book *Life with Picasso*, written with Carlton Lake, she puts it very simply: "My physical appearance did not seem extraordinary to me; on the other hand, I did not consider it a handicap. I felt afraid of nothing."[1]

What a gift. Considering that scarcely a woman lives who is not discontented with some aspect of her face or body, to be totally comfortable and contented with one's appearance is a rare and enviable quality.

This absolute self-belief was apparent as we sat and talked in the sunny living room adjoining her huge two-story studio with soaring windows facing north. The apartment is on a unique tree-lined street of buildings designed for artists, each containing luxurious combinations of studios and living quarters. There is no resemblance here to the romantic but seedy artisan's garret. These facilities were obviously created for the affluent rather than struggling artist.

Françoise Gilot is a successful painter who has been exhibiting her work for almost fifty years. When I arrived, some canvases were being removed from her studio in preparation for a show. She is the author of six books and has illustrated others. A few days later, I attended a lecture she gave at

Columbia University on the occasion of the publication of her latest book, *Matisse and Picasso: A Friendship in Art*, published by Doubleday, which was followed by a reception to view the exhibition of her most recent monotypes. She had her first exhibition when she was twenty-one, at the time she met Picasso.

"What attracted you to him?" I asked her. She tossed back her head and laughed.

Françoise Gilot poses with husband-to-be, polio vaccine pioneer Dr. Jonas Salk, June 1970 (he's 55, she's 48). *(AP/World Wide Photos)*

"You think women are attracted to men? No, it must be they who are attracted to you," she said emphatically. "Especially men who are gifted. Such a man knows what he wants." Then she smiled mischievously and added, "But I never wanted them. Not wanting them is the quality that makes them want you."

In her book, she describes the evening in 1943 when Picasso approached the table of the small Left Bank restaurant in which she was having dinner with two friends. He was with Dora Maar, the Yugoslavian photographer and painter who had been his companion since 1936 and whom he had painted in many variations. Françoise was with her girlfriend Genevieve, and the actor Alain Cuny, who was acquainted with Picasso. Although Genevieve was extremely beautiful, Picasso was immediately attracted to Françoise and invited both young women to come to his studio. At the beginning of their acquaintance, the talk was about art, but another side of his interest began to surface as Françoise continued to drop by his atelier.

"There were always quite a few people waiting to see him," she remembered in her book. "Picasso, I soon noticed, was always looking for some excuse to get me off into another room. . . . Whatever the pretext, it was quite clear that he was trying to discover to what degree I might be receptive to his attentions. I had no desire to give him grounds to make up his mind, one way or the other."[2]

What is startling about this account is the reserve and unconcern she evinces. Here is a neophyte painter being courted by the most famous artist of the time and not only is she unimpressed, she is virtually unresponsive. Most young women would have been awestruck and flattered beyond belief to have caught the fancy of this famous genius.

This sanguine self-possessed attitude toward greatness is one of the qualities that make Françoise Gilot unusually attractive to famous men. She treats them like mere mortals because she views them as such. She can take them or leave them, and often does. As she said to me with what I can only describe as a Gallic shrug, "I have said no many times. Oh yes, there have been many more *no's* than *yeses.*"

To a man who was accustomed to admiration and adoration, Françoise's cool indifference was at first puzzling and then challenging to Picasso, as described in this passage in her book:

He turned abruptly and kissed me, full on the mouth. I let him. He looked at me in surprise.

"You don't mind?" he asked. I said no—should I? He
seemed shocked. "That's disgusting," he said. "At least
you could have pushed me away. Otherwise I might get
the idea I could do anything I wanted to." I smiled and
told him to go ahead. By now he was thrown completely
off the track. I knew very well he didn't know what he
wanted to do—or even whether—and I had an idea that by
saying, placidly, yes, I would discourage him from doing
anything at all. So I said, "I'm at your disposition." He
looked at me cautiously, then asked, "Are you in love with
me?" I said I couldn't guarantee that, but at least I liked
him and I felt very much at ease with him and I saw no
reason for setting up in advance any limits to our relationship. Again he said, "That's disgusting. How do you expect me to seduce anyone under conditions like that? If
you're not going to resist—well, then it's out of the question. I'll have to think it over." And he walked back out
into the sculpture studio to join the others.[3]

You cannot fake that kind of poise and self-assurance, especially if you're an innocent twenty-one-year-old girl. The
cliché girl-gets-boy ploy of playing hard-to-get would be
transparently ineffective on a sexually sophisticated sixty-
year-old man. What drew him to this intelligent, unusual
young woman was not only the challenge but the comforting
familiarity of her inherent self-confidence.

Françoise Gilot walks through life carrying a core of personal strength and ego that the powerful recognize as kindred. She threatens no drain on their energies in order to
sustain herself; she is totally self-sufficient and will live side
by side with them without imposing the demands of a derivative existence. Adoration may be nice for a visit, but it is
hard to live with. Because she is highly intelligent and sees
herself as anyone's peer, the great man does not have to deal
with her insecurities, but rather finds her an easy and stimulating companion.

When Gilot told Picasso how much at ease she felt with him, "he grabbed my arm and burst out excitedly, 'But that's exactly the way I feel. When I was young, even before I was your age, I never found anybody that seemed like me. I felt I was living in complete solitude, and I never talked to anybody about what I really thought. I took refuge entirely in my painting. As I went along through life, gradually I met people with whom I could exchange a little bit and then a little bit more. And I had that same feeling with you—of speaking the same language. From the very first moment I knew we could communicate.' "[4]

Above all, Françoise offers to brilliant, achieving men the charm of the unattainable, because there is always that inner essence that they cannot reach: it is hers alone. She sat back on her couch, thoughtfully trying to frame her answer to my question of what is the secret of women who attract famous men, then came forth with this firm statement: "If a woman is her own person, the powerful man is attracted to her . . . to a person with her own center, her own window on the absolute. If I need him, then he doesn't need me. One of the qualities is having something of your own. If not, the man must carry around a dead weight." She stopped for a moment as if to gather her thoughts and then added slowly, "The secret is not being beautiful, there are many more beautiful; not charming, there are many more charming. The most important quality is to be independent and not need the man around all the time. Having one's own center is irreplaceable."

Could this be the complete answer . . . the feminine mystique that captures genius? Of course not. Even Françoise Gilot admits: "There is no recipe."

The components that go into attraction between the sexes are complex, as are the elements that go into the development of each human being. Ask a man what attracted him to a specific woman and he will probably mention a physical attribute. Ask a woman what special quality initially drew her to her husband or lover, and she will usually respond with a character trait that she found endearing. As a point of fact, neither of the above is the true reason for eliciting response but is merely a surface symbol of deeper qualities that create instant and instinctual emotional pulls between people.

The development of the unusual woman who is Françoise Gilot can be attributed in great part to her father and the interaction between them. By training as an agronomical engineer, M. Gilot built up several successful chemical-manufacturing companies. But he also had a passionate interest in literature. Disappointed because his only child was a daughter, he decided to ignore the fact and bring her up as though she were a son. Education and disciplined use of time dedicated to learning were the rules. By the time she was twelve, he had made her familiar with Poe, Rabelais and Baudelaire. She was given intensive riding lessons and became a skilled horsewoman. He decided she was to be an international lawyer and sent her to the Sorbonne, where she studied simultaneously for a license (equivalent to an American B.A.) in literature and for a law degree. Her days were carefully arranged so that every hour would be productive. This was a training that was to serve her for the rest of her life and enable her to handle the demands of a tyrannical Picasso while still finding time to continue her painting. Françoise adored and admired her father, but describes her relationship with him as "adversarial." He was a demanding, dictatorial and violent man who expected everyone to obey him immediately. She loved him deeply and admired his intelligence, but her powerfully independent spirit could not be crushed. She taught herself an effective technique of displaying deference when his demands were minor and defiance when they were major. As she described to me the way he tried to control her life, I could sense the relish she felt in fighting this little daily internecine war and the pride she developed as she found ways to win the battles. She yielded to his insistence on programming her days and planning her future because she was an excellent student who enjoyed schooling and did not feel that acquiescence to his imposed routines was damaging or demeaning, as long as his agenda did not conflict with hers.

"I learned that as long as I did what he wanted, I could also do what I wanted. My mother was phlegmatic, but rigid. As an only child, I could observe the relationship. I saw that she would not bend, and with a man like my father, that did not work. I was perceptive, and I recognized that it would be better to give him his way when it was not important. By the time I was fifteen, I could deal with my father much better than my mother could. Look, why am I a very good horsewoman? Because without thinking, I know what to do to make the horse do what I want. It is purely instinctive. The trick with everyone is looking in the mirror of the heart and putting yourself in the place of the other person."

Françoise started to paint at the age of seventeen and would cut morning classes at the university to study painting. But when she decided, at age twenty-two, that she wished to become a painter and give up her other studies, the days of acceding to her father were finished and her own strength and determination took over. When she told him that she planned to leave home and live life as a painter, he flew into an uncontrollable rage, as she knew he would. He beat her unmercifully, but she remained unmoved.

"He began to beat me, my head, shoulders, face and back with all his might," she wrote. "He was so much bigger and stronger than I, I knew I could never hold out against him if he continued like that. I sat down on the stairway and managed to slip my legs between the balusters. I put my arms through them and joined my hands together; in that way he couldn't hit my face anymore. My face was bleeding badly and the blood was running down the white balusters onto my knees. I could feel one eye swelling. He tried to pull me away but I held on tight."[5]

After that terrifying episode, he continued to try to thwart her plans by attempting to have her committed for psychiatric treatment. This was a man who was obsessive about achieving his own way. But he had met his match in his own daughter. French law requires that two independent psychiatrists concur in a judgment of insanity. Her father actually subjected Françoise to a round of examinations, but finally gave up when no doctor would find her anything but normal. She moved out of her parents' home and in with her grandmother and began painting.

The battle with her father not only formed her character, but prepared her for life with geniuses. She was quite accustomed to violent outbursts, erratic behavior, cruel criticism and tyrannical control. But Françoise was untouched by this abuse because she regarded it as unpleasant but impersonal, reflecting more on the abuser's character than hers. Her inner strength was unassailable, thanks to the incredibly cruel disciplinary training imposed by her father.

As a child, she was afraid of heights, a weakness her father would not permit. He forced her to climb up onto high rocks and jump down and paid no heed to her screams of fear. As soon as she accomplished one thing, he forced her to do something even harder, until her anger and resentment grew so intense that it left no room for fear. She was afraid of the water, so he forced her to swim, further and faster each time. By the time she was eight, she had become fearless and stoical and developed her own way to cope with his dictates. If there was something she wished to do that was likely to engender his disapproval, she would calmly work out in her own mind what the possible punishment would be and prepare herself to accept it. Thus she grew up to be a woman who was strong and totally sure of herself; she had been tried and tested over and over again and had emerged victorious. What better preparation for dealing with the demands of geniuses?

"Life with Pablo was a permanent roller coaster," wrote Françoise. "One day I would be praised to the sky, and the next morning find myself mercilessly criticized, as if I could do no right. My father's moods had been just as uneven, so I kept a measure of equanimity by thinking that when men were not excessive, they were usually mediocre."[6]

Here we see another major factor in explaining Françoise Gilot's unique qualifications to be the ideal mate of men of genius. She views intolerable behavior as a confirmation of a man's superiority. The only quality she will not forgive is mediocrity. She is able to maintain the posture of the strong, free female whom such a man wants because she does not regard catering to him as compromising her independence or feminist beliefs. In her view, emotional excesses are expected when one lives with brilliance.

"My father was difficult and immensely intelligent. That set a pattern for me," she told me. "I could not be attracted to men who were less than that. My father image was strong. He did not protect me. I would not like someone who would look upon me as an imp to be put into a bottle. I would not like that at all; I would break the bottle at once."

Françoise's liaison with Picasso lasted for ten years. The first eight were happy, albeit stormy. He was unfaithful more than once, which she accepted up to a point. Toward the end of 1952, she began to feel that their relationship was becoming meaningless. When he turned seventy, his escapades became more and more scandalous, and she became aware of his childishness and lack of equilibrium. That realization was "the crack that let in the light."[7] She had lost respect for the great man, and that for Françoise was the most important element in a relationship. When she announced to him that she was going to leave, he laughed off what he considered an empty threat. Who would leave the great Pablo Picasso? "No woman leaves a man like me," he said. "I told him maybe that was the way it looked to him, but I was one woman who would, and was about to. A man as rich and famous as he? He couldn't believe it, he said. I could only laugh at his complete misunderstanding of a woman with whom he had lived for so many years."[8] On September 30, 1953, Françoise left Picasso. He raged and raged, and never forgave her.

André Gide once told Picasso that Françoise was the kind of person who may have remorse but never regrets. When Picasso disagreed, Gide said, "It's easy to see that there's a dimension to her inner life which has escaped you."[9] When she visited him for the first time in 1944, Picasso told Françoise that he felt their relationship would bring light into both their lives. "My coming to him, he said, seemed like a window that was opening up and he wanted it to remain open. I did too, as long as it let in the light. When it no longer did, I closed it."[10]

On June 29, 1970, Françoise Gilot married Dr. Jonas Salk, perhaps the most famous scientist of this century. When I asked her what drew her to him, she said with a small laugh, "Nothing. The first few times we met, I did not even notice him. But *he* was attracted to me. What finally brought us together was architecture."

She explained that he had taken her to visit the Salk Institute, which is a magnificent collaboration between famed architect Louis Kahn and Dr. Salk.

"Jonas is tremendously interested in architecture," she said, "and as he described to me the features and elements of the buildings, right away there was a meeting of the minds."

Her eyes twinkled. "But it was not only minds. He is attractive. He is slim and elegant and has beautiful hands. Pablo was also attractive. Although he was an inch shorter than I, he had those incredible eyes."

She went on to describe her marriage to Salk, obviously a relationship that is highly satisfying to both of them. "True, if he had talked to me about science and I understood nothing, this would be bad. But thanks to my father, I had enough of a scientific background so that Jonas can talk to me about his work. Men with strong personalities demand more from their women. Only mediocre men ask for mothering.

But I believe to love is to be generous. You must try to understand them. If I fell in love with a baseball player, then I would learn baseball. It is not only good for the relationship, but you are enlarging your scope that way."

There again her credo, that genius entitles one to make selfish demands, and indeed, the lack of such assertions signifies that dreaded and disdained sin of mediocrity.

"Jonas and I spend about eight months of the year together. If I went with him to his meetings, what would I do? If he came to my exhibitions, what would he do? He is rewarded by the fact that I am famous, and as I am more and more known, he enjoys it. Such a man as Jonas must be his own person, and that person is self-confident. He wants other people to bloom beside him. I would never say 'yes' to a man who feels threatened by my work and success. If I think I would not be free, I would not accept. If two people are passionate about what they do, they are like stones that rub together and become smooth."

At this point in our talk, she jumped up to answer the phone and I noticed that she moved with the energy of a woman half her age and was startled to realize that I had not thought of her in terms of years at all. Her vitality and charm are ageless, and she is extraordinarily articulate, a quality she values.

"Many artists are dumb," she said as she came back and sat on the couch facing me. "They speak only through their art. Not so with Pablo. He was intelligent, witty, with very cogent ideas about art and the world. You could not resist his personality. Jonas is also very witty. He has philosophical interests and aspirations." She smiled. "You see, I am immune to simple charm."

Then I asked her how she could reconcile all her claims to independence with her statement that at the time she went to live with Picasso "I felt he was a person to whom I could, should devote myself entirely but should expect to receive nothing beyond what he had given the world by means of his art. I consented to make my life with him on those terms."[11]

She looked surprised and did not see that as any conflict in terms. "Both sexes are equal," she said, "but being equal doesn't mean you are the same. The archetype of man is a hunter; I have respect for that archetype. A woman cannot emasculate him by being the pursuer. For centuries, French women have maintained their importance by getting their way with implicit, rather than explicit, demands. We learn to let things go. To put vinegar on the relationship is bad, so we put oil. That doesn't mean we are subservient, it just means we have seen that oil works better. I let a man use his maximum ability to be himself and I will cater to that. But at the same time, he must do the same for me. We cater both to the other as persons to try to bring out the best in each of us."

She pointed out to me that Jonas Salk had spent two years learning to speak French fluently. "I never felt I gave up anything, ever. I devoted myself, yes, but I never gave up my painting. I do not put on a mask, I allow myself to have many moods, to be unpredictable. I think all my life men always liked my company because they can rely on me, they can talk to me. I don't have to be taken care of. Famous men don't have time to take care of women, and they don't need to be taken care of, because they have secretaries, managers. They want someone they can talk to, who will understand them, who will know what they are all about."

Militant feminists might quarrel with Françoise Gilot's referring to herself as a feminist, but definitions are personal. What one partner yields to the other in order to build a successful relationship is not male/female, it is person to person, friend to friend, and affects the giver only in terms of her vision of diminishment of self. If she does not see it as sacrifice but merely as reasonable accommodation, then her independence is not threatened.

That is the secret of Françoise Gilot. She was brought up by a father who taught her how to conquer the conquerors by whatever means were effective. She grew up in awe of no one and developed an unassailable sense of self-confidence because she had been tested and ultimately bested the man every child perceives as indestructible and all-knowing, her father. Combine this strength with a natural charm and the coquettish sexuality so many French women possess and you have a combination destined to appeal to great men. This is a woman with whom they can live comfortably, free to misbehave or behave aberrantly without guilt; this is a woman who remains untouched by their extravagant behavior because she is completely at ease with them and herself.

Françoise Gilot has lived and is living a remarkable life. In her earlier years, she lived on intimate terms with a mind-boggling list of legends of this century: Pablo Picasso, Georges Braque, Henri Matisse, Marc Chagall, André Gide, André Malraux, Fernand Léger, Jean Cocteau, Delacroix, Giacometti, Gertrude Stein. While we were chatting, I had a difficult time realizing we were talking about Pablo PICASSO and Jonas SALK. I can see where reverence can get in the way of relationships, and I can see that Françoise Gilot respects, but never reveres anyone. She offers a great man the stimulation of equality, the ease of nurturing a companionship and the sensual charm of a lovely woman who is totally secure in her femininity.

"Women," she said to me, "are different. We have imagination of the heart."

And that, perhaps, is the ultimate secret.

References

1. Françoise Gilot and Carlton Lake, *Life with Picasso*, New York/Toronto/London: McGraw-Hill Book Company, 1964, p. 27.
2. *Ibid.*, p. 21.
3. *Ibid.*, p. 24.
4. *Ibid.*, p. 32.
5. *Ibid.*, p. 30.
6. Françoise Gilot, *Matisse and Picasso: A Friendship in Art*, New York: Doubleday, 1990, p. 114.
7. Gilot and Lake, *op. cit.*, p. 347.
8. *Ibid.*, p. 354.
9. *Ibid.*, p. 252.
10. *Ibid.*, p. 367.
11. *Ibid.*, p. 335.

CHAPTER V

SLIM KEITH

The Three-Star Marrier
(Howard Hawks, Leland
Hayward, Sir Kenneth Keith)

*Charm is a woman's strength
just as strength is a man's charm.*
— Havelock Ellis,
The Task of Social Hygiene

TO READERS UNFAMILIAR with the remarkable men who became husbands of unremarkable Nancy "Slim" Gross of Salinas, California: Howard Hawks was a famed filmmaker in the freewheeling 1930s, when directors not only made movies but made stars as well (in more ways than one). Leland Hayward was the flamboyant agent who represented Greta Garbo, Henry Fonda, Fred Astaire and James Stewart in those same halcyon Hollywood days when such powerful men either slept with or married a steady series of beautiful women until they lost their power (again, in more ways than one). Kenneth Keith was a very wealthy Englishman who was knighted and became Sir Kenneth Keith (thus instantly transforming Nancy Gross into aristocratic Lady Keith).

Besides these spectacular marital acquisitions, Slim's along-the-way relationships sound like a name-dropper's idea of nirvana. The litany of luminaries with whom she either socialized or sexualized were from the legendary levels of the arts—literature, journalism, theatre, films and dance: Ernest Hemingway, Gary Cooper, Cary Grant, Clark Gable, William Randolph Hearst, Jerome Robbins, Truman Capote, William Paley and a list of lesser personalities who would have populated the pages of *People* magazine had it been published in the thirties, forties, and fifties. And if these liaisons do not convince you that Slim possessed some special magnetic qualities, here's a detail that is bound to impress all young men and women who came of age in this current era, which could well go down in history as the Age of Noncommitment: every one of Slim's three husbands proposed marriage by their third meeting. When you consider that these days men agonize over a New Year's Eve date for fear it could portend serious involvement, her triple-play achievement is awesome.

Not bad for a tall, skinny, athletic California-pretty high school dropout whose formal education ended in the middle of her senior year at a Dominican convent, when she decided that her interests lay more in living than learning. She had no career ambitions, no desire to change the world or improve the human condition; all she wanted to do was have the time of her life all of her life, a goal she achieved with stupendous success.

The question we all want answered is: how the hell did she do it?

Nancy Gross was born in Salinas, California, on July 15, 1917, to a sweet, compliant mother and a rigid, bigoted Germanic father whom, in her autobiography, *Slim*, she describes as an oppressive nonpracticing Catholic who hated and distrusted everyone and was politically somewhere to the right of Attila the Hun. She was the middle child, a position viewed by psychologists as the roughest sibling spot, accorded neither the status of the eldest nor the fond indulgence of the youngest. Nancy was boxed in between a beautiful, popular older sister who treated her with cruel disdain and a younger brother who was idolized by their father. Classically, this limbo position can either cripple one's self-esteem or drive one to prove superiority. As she describes in her book, Slim elected to take the high road: "All this humiliation could have turned into self-hatred. But I was lucky. Instead of hating myself, I began to hate my sister. Luckier still, that hatred took the form of strength and determination. I was determined not just to get even but to excel. I would be better, brighter, more beautiful: I would become someone who would scale heights and realize all the dreams my sister and I both must have had. I knew I would realize them, and I knew she wouldn't."[1]

This powerfully revealing statement provides the keys to Slim's social success. She had a compelling need to reach specific goals, plus the training to be inured to the humiliation, rejection and rebuff that are the inevitable price to be paid in any drive to the top.

Tough, cold, pushy—that's the way you might envision such an individual. Not Slim. She was likable, fun-loving and light-hearted but perceptive enough to evaluate her given assets and put them to use effectively. She realized that if these qualities could fly in Fresno, it might not be such a bad idea to bring them to a more exalted social arena, like Hollywood.

Certain that school did not offer the preparation she needed to achieve her coveted goals, she convinced her doting mother to allow her to drop out of the convent and to subsidize a sybaritic safari to a fancy resort where she could encounter LIFE. She chose a posh Death Valley resort where, as luck would have it, she ran into William Powell and Warner Baxter, two very hot movie stars who were vacationing there at the time. The three struck up one of those resort relationships where you spend every day together, develop a close friendship, swear to keep in touch when you get back to Real Life, and then usually never see each other again. But young Nancy had the invaluable instinct to be able to evaluate what men found attractive in her and to play the desired role in order to capitalize on their interests. Sophisticated, debonair William Powell, who was used to the tough tootsies of Tinseltown, was charmed by this wide-eyed, refreshingly ingenuous eighteen-year-old girl whom he dubbed "Slim Princess," the name that was thereafter shortened to "Slim." Instead of allowing the new friendship to fade into the usual post-vacation neglect, Slim managed to extend the valuable relationship so that Powell invited her and her mother to lunch at his home in Beverly Hills. When she saw his palatial, pillared mansion, Slim knew she had found the life she wanted and was determined to become part of the exciting, opulent playground of Hollywood.

From 1935 to 1938, Slim lived with her mother in Carmel, California, all the time circling L.A. and working on ways to get in. While most eighteen-year-olds were either going to secretarial school or college, she was studying with legendary restaurateur and bogus Russian prince Mike Romanoff, who taught her the techniques of piercing the Hollywood hierarchy. Then she met a young well-connected Harvard-schooled Virginian who was equally eager to enter the glamorous Hollywood circuit, and through him she finally made the big breakthrough via an invitation to a huge bash at William Randolph Hearst's gigantic "Tara by the Sea" in Santa Monica. This was her golden opportunity and she did not muff it; her now superbly honed social-climbing instincts led her to perform flawlessly as the perfect party guest and receive the ultimate reward of a follow-up invitation to the fabled San Simeon. William Randolph Hearst was one of the most powerful publishers in the country at the time. His sensational relationship with actress Marion Davies, for whom he had built the splendid castle, involved him with Hollywood, and movie stars were constantly in attendance at the spectacular parties at his weirdly dazzling replica of a European palace. Here Slim met Cary Grant and David Niven and eventually found her way into the Hollywood set. Only nineteen years old, she had discovered that you do not have to be a star to mingle with stars, you just have to be a visible peer; once seen at their social functions, acceptance is automatic. Slim's highly sensitive antennae quickly picked up on the fact that most movie stars' charming screen personalities are written for them; in real life they are deadly dull. An interesting, lively, pretty young woman offered a desirable contribution to their festivities. Soon she was dating B-movie actor Bruce Cabot (the one who saved Fay Wray from the clutches of King Kong) and dining with Cary Grant. She was now ready for the major move.

While twirling around the dance floor of a fashionable gambling house/nightclub one night with Albert Broccoli, who later went on to become the millionaire producer of the James Bond films, Slim saw Howard Hawks enter from the gambling room, where she much later learned he spent a good part of his life and livelihood. She managed to catch his eye and he came over to her companion, whom he knew, and asked for an introduction. Slim recognized the handsome, prematurely-white-haired man as one of Hollywood's hottest directors and knew that every aspiring young actress was a round-heeled pushover for him. When he opened with the corny casting-couch preamble that usually had them swooning in submission—"Do you want to be in movies?"—she airily answered, "No." He was intrigued.

Shrewd move number one: a good way to catch him is by surprise. When you're in the business of snaring a man, it is imperative to develop an array of tactics and the sharpness to size up your prospect swiftly in order to know which gambit to use. Slim obviously decided that the approach to use with jaded men was a facade of cool disinterest. Bull's-eye!

In actuality, Slim had neither aspirations for any sort of career nor ambition to do any sort of work. She did not want a big job, she wanted a BIG LIFE, and she saw Howard Hawks as the perfect passport. She immediately fell in love with him and what he offered and was determined to capture his interest. Remember that these were the days when flashy, voluptuous Betty Grable was the pin-up queen, when the leading stars were women with show-business backgrounds such as Barbara Stanwyck and Joan Crawford (in whose past there was reputed to be the business of showing much more than her background) and others whom you might hesitate to take to state dinners for fear they would shake hands with the butler and eat peas with their spoons. Slim offered the contrast of a convent-schooled, well-brought-up young woman who had all the upper-class accomplishments of riding, shooting and hostessing, plus the lean and hungry look enshrined by *Vogue*; she had style, elegance and class, qualities in very short supply in L. A. in those years.

Howard Hawks had become famous for developing a female ideal that was unique in the 1930s. Instead of the usual clinging, coy, submissive girl featured in films of the day, he introduced slim, sassy, competent, independent women such as Katharine Hepburn, Rosalind Russell and Lauren Bacall— the kind of women who look great in shirt and pants while riding and hunting with their men during the day and are breathtakingly feminine in a flowing ball gown on the dance floor at night. Nancy Gross was exactly this sort of woman. You could say she was lucky that she met the right man at the right time, but I don't buy that. I subscribe to the conveyor-belt theory of life, which postulates that all people are presented with a stream of opportunities that continue to pass along during our lifetimes. Only some of us have the vision to recognize these opportunities, the brains to reach out and grab the right one and the guts to make it into something. All those less imaginative, timid bystanders enviously attribute the winner's success to luck, but luck is merely an alibi created by the losers of the world.

Slim was presented with a golden opportunity when she encountered Howard Hawks, but if she had not met him that fateful night, she would have gone on until she met another Mr. Powerful. This was a young woman determined to inject herself into the top echelons of society and become Mrs. Somebody, no matter what it took.

On their first date, she learned that he had three children and a wife (Norma Shearer's sister) who was in a loony bin. His oldest child was only seven years Slim's junior, he was twenty-two years older than she, and California law prohibited divorcing a mentally incompetent spouse. On the plus side, however, we have the powerful position, the big house, the four cars, the butler and the yacht—in Slim's own words, "exactly the package I wanted."[2] Marriage to Howard Hawks was obviously a goal worth working toward, and Slim was determined.

This is where the ability to handle humiliation and rejection and the will to win become the powerful weapons needed to capture the big matrimonial prize. For three years Slim's relationship with Hawks put her in the demeaning role of "the other woman," a position she clung to while hoping and pushing for him to be able to divorce his wife. Today the image of an unmarried couple living and traveling together is ho-hum conventional. But in the 1930s, such liaisons were regarded as scandalous and the woman was looked upon as a tarnished hussy. Slim had to undergo some scorn and lifted eyebrows, maybe even a little pity and contempt. But she was used to harsh, often punitive treatment from her father and sister and had learned to remain untouched by it. She tried to preserve the proprieties somewhat by living at home with her mother, but traveled everywhere with Hawks, which made him even more desirable to the determined young girl, who wanted to be part of his world of the rich and famous. "Everywhere" with Howard Hawks meant trips to Key West to visit with Ernest Hemingway, dinners with Rosalind Russell and Gary Cooper—heady stuff for the kid from Salinas. But she knew what she wanted and was willing to risk the so-called "best years of her life." Persistence finally paid off, and on December 11, 1941, twenty-four-year-old Nancy Gross married Howard Hawks and was led down the aisle by Gary Cooper to begin her bigger-than-life LIFE.

First came the fantasy house built by the architect of the Pasadena Rose Bowl. She furnished it from top to bottom with no expense spared, including dressing-room shelves filled with hundreds of shoes, handbags and sweaters. Then came the sharing of Hawks's career, which involved his asking her to read scripts. She did the job well except for rejecting the one called *Everybody Goes to Rick's*, which turned out to be *Casablanca*.

She was now part of the fabulous glamour world of which she had dreamed. But eventually the blinders came off. Howard Hawks was an incurable gambler. There were constant threats of knee-breaking to encourage payment of astronomical debts to his bookie. He was also a liar who claimed to have performed all sorts of daring feats. He said he was a stunt flier, but could barely steer an airplane. Aboard his yacht he became the heroic commander when he wasn't puking his guts out over the side. At the racetrack, he came on as a great Kentucky horse breeder but never owned a stable. Apparently he was a man who not only created fantasies on the screen but in real life as well. He was also an accomplished womanizer, and his wife had to contend with a stream of starlets and endless broken promises.

I asked a friend of Slim's why Slim never noticed these major character deficiencies before marriage. After all, she had spent three years with him, traveled with him, lived with him. How could she have been unaware of such flagrant behavioral transgressions?

"When you want something very much, maybe you delude yourself . . . you close your eyes a bit," Slim's friend answered. She went on to explain that Slim never had the small dreams of the conventional young girl of her day, marrying the handsome high school football hero who would carry her off to the rose-covered cottage where she would live the middle-American dream of PTA meetings and two-week vacations at the lake. She wanted an extraordinary life —the elegant, glamorous existence that most teenagers moon over in movie magazines and regard as an unattainable celluloid fantasy. Nancy Gross realized after meeting William Powell that she could attract movie stars just as easily as home-team heroes. She went for it and that "it" meant Howard Hawks, warts and all. And the easiest way of dealing with the warts was developing a blind eye.

At no point did Slim live any other than a derivative life. The only achievements she could ever claim were reading scripts for Hawks and discovering Lauren Bacall for the starring role in *To Have and Have Not*, the definitive Bogart-Bacall film. She liked furnishing and running nice homes for her men and enjoyed playing the smart and decorative hostess. Of course, it's not too hard to have a successful party when your guest list includes Moss Hart, Samuel Goldwyn, Tyrone Power and Darryl Zanuck.

It sounds great, but after a while one realizes that a poker game is a poker game, whether it's played by Robert Capa, Lew Wasserman and Constance Bennett or by Benny Ginsberg, the salesman, and Tommy O'Connor, the mechanic from down the hall, and once the glamour curtain is lifted, you're still spending your life with a bunch of schmucks. The only difference between rich and poor marriages is that only the financially secure can afford the luxury of complaining about emotional deprivation. When you're scrubbing, cleaning, cooking and struggling to pay bills, there's not much opportunity to sit around munching bonbons and pondering the quality of life. On the other hand, there's only so much pleasure you can get from riding your horse around your vast estate every afternoon and ordering the servants around.

It was time for Slim to become aware of her husband's coldness and lack of emotion, and her resultant loneliness. By 1944, just three years after the gloriously victorious all-white storybook wedding, she knew that the marriage was a bust. Of course, life wasn't all that bad and Slim was now part of the world she had longed and fought for, but not even Palm Springs in the winter and croquet on the lawn with Douglas Fairbanks, Jr. could offset the deteriorating effect of her husband's constant infidelities and continual absences.

Many an unhappy, betrayed wife has assuaged her bruised ego with a little lustful byplay with the milkman or a small libidinous plunge with the plumber. But how about some fun with Clark Gable? He was the "King of Hollywood," the handsome heartthrob of the era, the heroic Major Clark Gable who had returned from the war with a Distinguished Flying Cross. His wife and great love of his life, the beautiful film star Carole Lombard, had been killed in a plane crash in 1942, and the newspapers had been filled with pictures of the grief-stricken Gable flying to the site of the tragedy in hopes of finding her alive.

When most housewives of the forties answered the doorbell, they probably found the Fuller Brush man or a guy selling vacuum cleaners. But if you traveled in Slim's circles, Clark Gable could turn up on your doorstep one day. And that's just what happened. He dropped by to find out about Howard Hawks's motorcycle club, and a small flirtation began that blossomed into a relationship. She described it as a tantalizing but never carnal relationship that kept her spirits up until she found out that she was pregnant with Howard Hawks's child.

Her daughter, Kitty, was born in February 1946. The occasion was apparently no great thrill to Howard, as he already had three children, and he took off for business as usual. Although in her book she professes to have been delighted with the prospects of motherhood, the reality did not seem to present the anticipated pleasure. In April, she left her two-month-old daughter and headed for a glorious two weeks of fun and frolic in New York, with rounds of cocktail parties and dancing the nights away at El Morocco, followed by a week in Nassau and then a week or two in Cuba visiting with the Ernest Hemingways, spiced up with such drop-in visitors as William Paley, Leland Hayward and his wife, Mar-

garet Sullavan, and David Selznick and his wife, actress Jennifer Jones. Not a bad way to handle postpartum depression.

When I interviewed Slim's friend, I mentioned that in
later years, Slim spoke of her daughter as the finest achievement in her life and undeniably the most wonderful girl in
the world: Slim must have turned into a great mother. The
reaction I got was total silence. When I mentioned that I
might want to interview Kitty, the cryptic comment was, "I
wouldn't." Protestations of daughterly perfection and the
joys of motherhood notwithstanding, the picture presented
in Slim's autobiography is of a self-centered hedonist whose
first concern was to go where the fun folk were whenever
the opportunity arose and the nanny or boarding school
would take care of the kid. Once when she was invited to
some holiday hoopla with some of the beautiful people, she
lied to her two-year-old, pretending that Christmas fell on
December twenty-third and going through the whole gift-
giving, tree-lighting shtick two days early so that she could
be away over Christmas. Only a nonparenting parent could
believe that a two-year-old child is too young to be aware
that her friends are celebrating Christmas two days later.

By 1946 the routine of days around the pool and evenings
spent partying with Hollywood stars and moguls was losing
its appeal and novelty. It was time for a big change. Enter
Leland Hayward.

A forever-boyish-looking man with a crew cut, tremendous enthusiasm, great blue eyes and what everyone described as an electric personality, Leland Hayward was one
of the wonder boys of Broadway and Hollywood. He had
flunked out of Princeton at the end of his freshman year and
started in show business as a press agent for United Artists.
He had begun his marital career by marrying a debutante
whom he divorced, remarried and divorced again. When
talkies began in 1927, he had the prescience to realize that
Hollywood would need professional writers and stage actors
who had trained voices, and he convinced the American Play

Company to set up a movie department that would represent writers and actors. A few years later, he went out on his own and built up one of the most prestigious rosters of clients in the country, sold that to MCA and became a producer, subsequently turning out such Broadway hits as John Hersey's *A Bell for Adano*, Lindsay and Crouse's *State of the Union*, *South Pacific*, *Mister Roberts*, and *Gypsy*, as well as movies such as *Red River* with John Wayne and Montgomery Clift. He was a vital, exciting man who didn't care much for outdoor sports but was a hot number with such indoor activities as womanizing. Years before he and Slim met, he had broken off an affair with Katharine Hepburn to marry Margaret Sullavan, who was now the mother of his three children.

Slim encountered Leland at a party she'd gone to with Howard at the Selznicks'. He was there solo, as wife Margaret preferred the East Coast. As Slim tells it, there was a powerful instant attraction leading to a blazing affair that soon became common gossip in Hollywood.

A little thing like a wife and three young children seemed to present no impediment to Slim, or apparently to Leland either. Again, she saw what she wanted and she reached for it. Already experienced in winning away married men, Slim viewed the breaking up of Leland Hayward's marriage as merely inconvenient. The wife is easy; you brush her off with the excuse that she had neglected her husband, failed to give him the love and attention he needed, and thus deserved to lose him. But how do you deal with the problem of the bereft family? In this case, there were three little children who adored their father and were devastated by his defection, as described by daughter Brooke Hayward in her best-selling book, *Haywire*. And how do you assuage the guilt suffered by Leland for imposing on his children the same searing sense of abandonment that had been inflicted upon him when he was a child by his own father, which he claimed he swore never to do to his offspring? Margaret Sullavan hated California and preferred to maintain a home in Connecticut—a wonderful, big white house that the children loved. Leland's work was on two coasts, so he was continually flying in and out. The way Slim saw it, poor Leland was being neglected and his wife should have moved around with him. Of course, that would have meant constantly abandoning the children, but in Slim's mind kids were of secondary importance. Pleasing a husband was not only more fun, but to a wife's ultimate best interests. She herself went off frequently with Leland, leaving Howard, who barely noticed being left, and little daughter Kitty, who was in the hands of a nanny. Slim was madly in love with Leland Hayward and she would have him at any cost.

We see evidence of little Nancy Gross's intuitive ability to develop the persona demanded by the man she desired. With William Powell, she was the healthy, outdoor ingenue; with Howard Hawks, she was elegant, elusive Slim; now with Leland Hayward, she became the intelligent, independent public personality he preferred. At that time, *Harper's Bazaar* was making a big to-do about the all-American "California Girl," and Slim Hawks became their much-publicized symbol of the long and tawny look worthy of worship. Leland liked a woman who had her own identity, and Slim appeared to have that, although it was clearly a role with which she was not comfortable. When publicly accepting the Neiman-Marcus fashion award, she froze and could not deliver the speech that had been written for her by a most unusual duo of speechwriters, playwrights Lindsay and Crouse.

In June 1949, their divorces out of the way, Slim and Leland were married in the garden of the Manhasset estate of Bill and Babe Paley. Slim had moved from the glittering cast of Hollywood to join the establishment of the Eastern elite. Now her days and evenings were spent with Josh and Nedda Logan, Marion and Irwin Shaw, Richard and Dorothy Rodgers, Mary Martin, Kitty and Moss Hart. Babe Paley became her closest female friend, and Truman Capote, her closest male friend. (That friendship blew up when he wrote his devastating caricatures of Slim and Babe in "La Côte Basque," from the unfinished novel *Answered Prayers*, and excerpted in *Esquire* magazine in 1975.)

The twelve years she spent with Leland Hayward were the happiest years in Slim's life. She loved the cachet of being Mrs. Leland Hayward and the exciting world of America's top creative people to which her derivative identity admitted her. She adored the pointless, vacuous days of alcoholic luncheons in socially approved boîtes with friends, gossiping about the friends she'd lunched with the day before. In true theatrical style, she claims an inventory of famous "dearest friends" so extensive as to convey the image of either a person who must devote the major portion of her time to ministering to these many intimate relationships, or one who hasn't a clue as to the real meaning of friendship.

And now we come to the part of this story that could be entitled "What goes around comes around," or "How people who do unto others sometimes get undone."

In 1959, Pamela Churchill (divorced wife of Winston's son Randolph) took a fancy to Leland Hayward and in the so-who-cares-if-he's-married style of their social circle, lured him away and made Slim into the newest ex-Mrs. Hayward. The fact that she was able to do it with such ease is perhaps due to Slim's misconception of the requisites of a happy marriage and the natural giving each spouse does merely out of love. Here's how Slim put it in her book: "If you have any conscience or spirit or soul or goodness in you at all, you help a mate get through his troubles. Maybe in a different marriage, I could have had that compassion. Unfortunately, I'd been drawing on a dwindling supply of it for a long, long time; and when all you can do, over and over, is sympathize with sick children and a beleaguered husband, you stop, at some point, thinking about them and start wondering where you're going to get some relief."[3]

When I asked one of Slim's friends how so savvy a woman could not see the signs of discontent that made her husband vulnerable to a hostile takeover, the friend answered with a rueful smile, "She told me that her big mistake was that she just wasn't paying attention."

Just as Slim had taken advantage of Margaret Sullavan's neglect of Leland, so Pamela Churchill moved in when she detected the signs of a man who was not getting properly serviced. When Slim finally woke up and realized the situation, she tried to salvage her marriage with the recommendation to her husband that he have an affair with Pamela, as popular gossip indicated had already occurred with a string of other prominent men, but keep intact what she considered to be their happy marriage.

"But whatever you do, for your own protection, for your own dignity, don't marry her," Slim advised her husband. "You don't have to. Nobody *marries* Pamela Churchill. Gianni Agnelli didn't do it. Elie de Rothschild didn't do it, Edward Murrow didn't do it. Why should you?"[4]

Strange counsel for a wife to give a husband. But Slim was a paradox with one foot in one generation and one in another and an olio of mixed moralities. Why is it undignified to marry a woman who has had lovers? Does this imply that the poor, used wretch who has been cast off by men is too tarnished to bear the honor of your name? And why did Slim take the conventional macho position that presumes the woman to be the rejectee rather than the rejector? Her strange ethical code saw no wrongdoing in committing adultery; in fact, she admitted that she too had wandered on occasion during their marriage. The fact that she was discreetly cuckolding her husband and that he had little sideline flings was acceptable. She saw these activities as small entertainments and no threat. But marriage? That's a big-deal, public, till-death-or-divorce-do-us-part commitment. Besides, no man should demean himself by marrying a woman who has been sleeping with half the power structure in the Western world.

Nevertheless, in 1959 Slim Hayward found herself unexpectedly single. Again, let's point out the difference between the real world and Slim's. The cast-off divorcée today goes to her local support group in order to get sympathy from other women who have been similarly dumped. Slim was suffering the same pangs of sadness, but her moral support came in the form of a phone call to her room at the Ritz in Paris from Ernest (Hemingway), followed by a cable from Jerry (Jerome Robbins), who was then choreographing at the Spoleto Festival and who suggested that she come visit him. After her stay in Spoleto, she went off to watch the running of the bulls in Pamplona with Papa Hemingway. I'm not saying that Slim was not suffering from a broken heart and a sense of rejection, but you have to admit that the pain is a lot easier to take when you're sobbing into your sangria in Seville with Papa Hemingway than when you're dropping tears in your tea in your friend Irma's Brooklyn kitchen.

For the first time in her life, Slim was without a caretaker. She was a woman who had always depended upon others to take charge of her life. In that sense she was little different from widows and divorcées who lead sheltered, protected and derivative existences and suddenly find themselves afloat and, in effect, out of a job.

Enter a handsome English banker named Kenneth Keith. Slim met him on a blind date in New York and then resumed the friendship when she took a flat in London for two months in the summer of 1960. Wealthy, the owner of a Bentley, a private plane and a huge country estate, he proposed marriage to her on about their third date. Slim was not in love with him and didn't find him exciting, but in her view, only marriage could convey upon a helpless female the dignity and position that enabled her to hold her head up. And he was a great catch. So they were married.

But why did he marry her? Just as she needed social validation, apparently so did he. Kenneth Keith was a powerful executive whose entire life was business. He had no friends, merely colleagues. His elegant home was furnished with the impersonality of a Hilton Hotel suite. He did not need a wife to breed heirs; he already had two children. He was by then one of the most prominent men in England, but one of the least popular, having apparently chilled a lot of people on his way up. He could have had his pick of luscious young bimbos. But what he required in his exalted position was a decorative, competent hostess who could run his homes well and fill them with interesting people, who could add the dimension of an elegant, distinctive social life to his narrow existence and soften his public image. Slim presented the perfect package. She knew everyone, was socially acceptable in the highest circles, was smart-looking and elegant.

Keith's choice was much the same as those made by Saul Steinberg and John Gutfreund in America, who were like frogs looking for pretty girls to kiss them and turn them into princes. Men who have been brutal sons of bitches in their ruthless drives upward often find it lonely and boring at the top. Suddenly they decide to alter their images, to become popular social lions and benefactors of the same mankind they have been shafting and exploiting for years. They have money, they have power, now they want to be loved.

The difference between Keith and his American counterparts was that an upwardly mobile Englishman must have a wife who can sit a horse, shoot well and know how to handle the servants. Talents required by the billionaire New York network run more to the ability to commit extravagant ostentation and be savvy enough to know that fellatio is not a new pasta dish.

Slim fulfilled her part of the bargain well. She redecorated the houses and turned them into homes. She held entertaining dinner parties where people actually had a good time. And then came the capping of Kenneth's career: he was awarded a knighthood. Suddenly, he was Sir Kenneth and little Nancy Gross was Lady Keith. It was quite a coup for the kid from Salinas; one would hope that her wicked sister was green with envy. However, the title did not compensate for her loveless existence. Not only did Slim not love Sir Kenneth, she didn't even like him.

Slim had dreams, she had drive, she had determination, but as one of her friends said, she had standards. She was, I am told, willing to make many compromises and did, but one area in which she would not compromise was love. When she stopped loving Howard Hawks, she left him for Leland Hayward. When she tried living with Sir Kenneth, a man she did not love, she found it intolerable and so she divorced him.

That's the way Slim tells it. She and her friends probably believe it. The way I see it, her only standards were boredom and self-interest. She lived with Howard Hawks for loveless years, but they were exciting times filled with glamorous, interesting people, not to mention titillating amours, and she needed the status of being Mrs. Hawks, not to mention the money, to keep her place in Hollywood society. By the time she got to Kenneth Keith, she no longer needed the status and she no longer needed the money. True, she would have been wealthier had she stayed Lady Keith, but she owned her apartment at the Pierre Hotel on Fifth Avenue and she had enough money to buy whatever she wanted and travel wherever she wished. She already knew all the people she had married men to meet, so her social life was secure. At this point in her life, Kenneth Keith had little to offer her, and living his rigid country English life was a boring pain in the ass to a woman who was used to living the freewheeling life of Hollywood and New York.

Slim Keith died in April 1990. She had started life as a rather ordinary girl with no apparent qualities that would mark her as a candidate for the life she ultimately lived. What she had was an enormous amount of style and the shrewdness to recognize how to use her innate individuality to reach the pinnacles to which she aspired. She coolly and consciously calculated her assets and worked out ways to use them to achieve success the easy way—by marrying it rather than earning it. Nancy early on recognized that she had the ability to play people, men especially. She instinctively recognized which button to press to make them respond, which image of her they preferred. By the time she met Kenneth Keith, her personality was working on automatic pilot and she unconsciously became the wife he sought, just as she had with Howard Hawks and Leland Hayward. Today, such talents, combined with an M.B.A., could take her to the top of the corporate world, but in Slim's day women used their abilities to become the companions of men who would take that path. If she had been born forty years later, Slim Keith might have been the first female president of IBM. But she wouldn't have had as much fun.

References

1. Slim Keith with Annette Tapert, *Slim*, New York: Simon & Schuster, 1990, p. 28.
2. *Ibid.*, p. 60.
3. *Ibid.*, p. 254.
4. *Ibid.*, p. 251.

Pamela Harriman, in April 1977. *(AP/World Wide Photos)*

CHAPTER VI

PAMELA DIGBY CHURCHILL HAYWARD HARRIMAN

The Class-Act Man-Catcher

A man says what he knows,
a woman says what will please.
—Jean-Jacques Rousseau,
Du Contrat Social

"SHE LOOKS LIKE AN IRISH BARMAID!" said the woman contemptuously.

"She's sensual, lovely and *very* attractive," said the man dreamily.

"She's a fancy whore!" said the woman angrily.

"She's a great courtesan—she makes a man feel wonderful," said the man with a fond, faraway smile.

They were both speaking about Pamela Harriman, which gives you an idea of the gender gap in opinions about this famous red-haired English aristocrat who has racked up a glittering record of lovers and husbands, and who now reigns in Washington as the grande dame of the Democratic party.

First catch, Randolph Churchill (Winston's son); second, Leland Hayward (Slim's husband); third, Averell Harriman (who left her $75 million). In between, love affairs with Aly Khan, Elie de Rothschild, Gianni Agnelli, Jock Whitney, Ed-

ward R. Murrow, Stavros Niarchos. If you were very rich
and/or famous and/or powerful, you were Pamela's meat;
extant wives were no deterrent. A close friend said of her in
Marie Brenner's July 1988 article in *Vanity Fair*, "We used to
say about Pamela that if you put a blindfold on her in a
crowded room, she could smell out the powerful men."[1]
When she spotted her prey, she handled conquests like any
Wall Street raider with the boldness of a Boesky and the
morality of a Milken. Each of her acquisitions was immediately restructured and divested of all prior commitments,
such as children and old friends. She then proceeded to remake his life into her own creation; he had to be the sole
property of Pamela, but the world she set him up in was so
comfortable and pleasurable that it was well worth the price
to him. His family, of course, felt differently.

As you can gather, Pamela is not universally loved. In
writing this chapter, I found that the roster of people, mostly
women, who haven't a kind word to say for Pamela to be
longer than Nixon's enemies list. And the number who
would gladly talk about her but insisted they not be quoted
was even more extensive; $75 million carries a lot of clout.
When Brooke Hayward, Pamela's stepdaughter by marriage
number two, voiced very strong opinions to a writer for *W*,
suggesting that Pam better withdraw her application for the
Stepmother-of-the-Year Award, Brooke received an immediate call from big-bucks attorney Edward Bennett Williams
warning that she had best cease and desist or high-cost legal
unpleasantness could befall her. Of course, Brooke had already done a number on Pam in *Haywire*.

Women do not seem to like Pamela Harriman, but men
adore her, which probably accounts for much of the female
antagonism. It is aggravating to watch another woman mes-
merize a man before your eyes; you want to punch his lights
out for being such a pushover and you want to rip out her
carefully coiffed red hair for knowing how to charm him.
Her conquests have required skill, knowledge and practice,

and those she certainly has. Her refusal to be interviewed for this book was probably based on sex—I am the wrong one. She has endured enough hatchet jobs in articles by women writers.

Pamela Digby was the first-born child of a minor English baron, Lord Digby, who dairy farmed and grew rhododendrons in the vast gardens of Minterne, their stately home near Dorchester. She grew up in conventional upper-class comfort: riding, hunting, learning French from governesses and little else, as lords and ladies of the day did not believe in formal education for young women. As in all aristocratic families, the children saw very little of their parents, and from all reports, the kids didn't miss much. "The Digbys were almost cartoon peers who seemed to come from the pages of *Punch*," said William Walton, a *Time-Life* correspondent during World War II. But Pamela had far grander dreams for her life than spreading manure on flower beds and bringing baskets to the poor on Christmas.

"My sister Pamela decided early on she was going to turn herself into a very glamorous person," Sheila Digby Moore told Marie Brenner. Pamela's role model was not her mother, whom Sheila describes as "a very forceful and difficult person,"[2] but more than likely a notorious nineteenth-century relative, Lady Jane Digby, who was included in a book called *The Wilder Shores of Love*, a 1954 study by Lesley Blanch of history's great courtesans. Apparently Lady Jane didn't hide her light under a bushel but chose to go so public with her illicit antics that she achieved the dubious distinction of being denounced as an adulteress on the august floor of the House of Lords. She was not the sort of ancestor boasted of in aristocratic drawing rooms.

"Our aunts couldn't bear it when we would discuss Jane Digby," Sheila Moore said in the *Vanity Fair* article, "but Pamela was always intrigued by her"[3] and still has a bracelet that ostensibly belonged to her. Pamela's interest in her colorful antecedent has reportedly resulted in weekend guests being treated to readings from *The Wilder Shores of Love*, either out of desperation or inspiration, one would assume, if the weekend is turning into a real drag. Pamela might have approved of Lady Jane's life-style, but she certainly would not have identified with her ultimate fate, which consisted of days and nights of Bedouin bliss washing the feet of an Arab prince, unless, of course, he promised to leave her his tent condo plus a fleet of camels.

There's a joke about the arriviste yachtsman who, when he asked his mother to address him as "Captain," was told, "By you you're a captain and by me you're a captain, but by a captain are you a captain?" By the standards of genuine English aristocracy, Lord Digby's barony was unimpressive. His was not one of the great ducal houses. Being the daughter of a minor aristocrat was undoubtedly something that bugged young Pamela, who aspired to reach more distinguished levels.

Pamela was not a great beauty, and tended toward plumpness in her youth and again in later years. However, she had lovely red hair and that wonderful English complexion; in her book, Slim Keith constantly refers to Pamela Harriman's famous white skin. In fact, every piece I read about her alludes to that white skin and famous white shoulders. In these days when winter tans are important evidence of upper-income sojourns in the sun and white skin is regarded as unhealthy-looking, it's hard to understand the paeans to her pale face. But along with her appearance, she had breeding, charm and intelligence, and a developing sense of how to put it all together to vault to the heights of power.

Her first big chance came when she was nineteen. In October 1939, Randolph Churchill, the twenty-eight-year-old son of Winston Churchill, then First Lord of the Admiralty, was given Pamela's name for a blind date. After three dates, they became engaged and were married a few weeks later.

Randolph was a renowned reprobate, a dissolute drunkard and what the English term an all-around rotter. A member of the famous White's Club, he had to be forcibly ejected many times for obnoxious behavior. Why would a young woman marry such a man? Nowhere has it ever been mentioned that she fell head over heels in love with him. What is more likely is that she did feel tremendously attracted to the great-grand-son of the seventh Duke of Marlborough and the son of the man slated to become prime minister. Fortunately, she did not have to deal with Randolph's fabled rudeness and irascibility for too long, as he was posted to Cairo within a month and left her, pregnant with the child who grew up to be Winston Churchill II, at present a minor member of Parliament. Shortly thereafter, her father-in-law became prime minister and she moved into 10 Downing Street during her pregnancy and became the pet of Winston Churchill.

Pamela had what they call "a very good war." She lived at the seat of power and started to develop her male-charming career with her father-in-law, whom she called "Papa." She set up a salon in her chic flat at 49 Grosvenor Square to entertain important men—rarely women, of course—General Eisenhower, William Paley, Jock Whitney, all the leading journalists and top-level Allied brass. Lord Beaverbrook, the famous newspaper magnate, became a close friend, a relationship that lasted until he died. Pamela soon discovered that she had an instinctive political sense, an invaluable asset that she learned to use wisely and well. Young as she was, Pamela recognized the value of her position and reveled in it. Winston Churchill not only became very fond of her, but obviously respected her; it was commonly believed that he trusted her subtly to convey and elicit information about the thinking processes of his ally, the United States, whose leaders did not always see eye to eye with him. By twenty-one, she was at the very pinnacle of power, a prominent member of London society, and had achieved the ultimate accolade of being chosen to grace the cover of *Life*, then the largest, most important magazine in the world, where she was pictured in a 1941 issue with her infant son.

In the published diaries of Sir Henry Channon (always known as "Chips," described by an English friend as "an enormously rich, snobbish American who had married a Guinness heiress") he writes on December 9, 1941, "I dined in with Harold [Nicholson] and the auburn alluring Pam Churchill. . . . Kathleen Harriman and her dark, distinguished father, Averell, also came and we drank one of my last magnums of Krug 1920." On December 6, 1942, he records, "Later I went to see Pam Churchill in her flat at 49 Grosvenor Square. While I was there Averell Harriman and Max Beaverbrook [owner of the *Daily Express* and minister for munitions] both rang up."

The war treated Pamela wonderfully, even to the point of eliminating the need to deal with the unpleasantness of her loutish husband, who was so universally unpopular that when he asked for a regimental transfer, his commanding officer told him how delighted they were to be rid of his loathsome presence. When Randolph did come home on leave, it was frequently reported that Pamela hated him so much that she apparently could not stand to be in the same room with him. Fortunately, the war kept him away much of the time, allowing her to play out the marvelous roles of upper-class, stiff-upper-lip war wife, loyal and beloved daughter-in-law of the most important man in England, and mother of that man's only grandson and namesake, a direct descendant of the Duke of Marlborough. She was no longer just minor nobility—Pamela Digby was now an intimate of the most powerful group in the world, the select cadre of national leaders who were, in effect, controlling the entire Allied war effort. Pamela Churchill was the only person in London to receive letters from three participants at the Yalta Conference. And she was only twenty.

Think of the picture she presented to these older, war-weary men who were flying in and out of London to confer at the highest levels of government. With her lovely red hair and alabaster skin, aristocratic bearing and breeding, she was not only deliciously fresh and young, but carried the cachet of the Churchill name and, reputedly, access to the prime minister's ear. By now she was highly skilled in the art of pleasing men and making them feel comfortable and desirable. Is it any wonder they all adored her? While the rest of the women in the world were living desolate and desperate man-less lives, Pamela Churchill had her pick of the best the United States and Great Britain had to offer.

Edward R. Murrow, the legendary CBS correspondent whose radio voice came to symbolize the war and whose television programs became models for later television journalism, was Pamela's real love of those years, according to her friends. They had a passionate affair, notwithstanding the presence in London of Janet Murrow, who was a friend of Clementine Churchill, Pamela's mother-in-law. There are many ways betrayed wives handle their husbands' infidelity; Janet's choice was to leave London, return to America and cut her husband off without a word. It turned out to be the wise course of action. Murrow was smitten with Pamela, but he was a moral man who was troubled by his own adulterous behavior. Not hearing from his wife exacerbated his feelings of guilt. According to a biography of Murrow by A. M. Sperber, his letters home began to contain pleas for forgiveness and reconciliation and avowals of love. It was assumed that Pamela wanted to divorce Randolph and marry Murrow, but this is mere conjecture and it is quite possible that she did not wish to leave her seat of power in London. However, this all became academic, because in the spring, Janet Murrow became pregnant at age thirty-five, after years of trying to have a baby, and the Murrows looked forward to joyful parenthood together.

Then along came another top-notch suitor, the very distinguished Averell Harriman. Forty-nine years old, extremely handsome, elegant and wealthy, this Groton-and-Yale educated heir to the Union Pacific Railroad fortune was sent over by President Roosevelt to organize the Lend-Lease Program. In later years, Pamela said, "He was the best-looking man I had ever seen." Harriman fell madly in love with Pamela, but Marie Harriman was another wife who was not easily removed. A millionaire-acquirer par excellence in her own right (her previous husband was Sonny Whitney, one of the richest men in the United States), she was a strong and savvy lady who was not about to lose her prized possession to a callow twenty-year-old. The possibility of Pamela marrying Harriman was also blocked by his reluctance to create a scandal and by his ambition to run for president, which would have been inconceivable in those days for a divorced man. When he left London to take up a post as American ambassador to Moscow, he is reported to have instructed his attorney to settle an allowance of $50,000 a year on Pamela, an amount so insignificant to him that he totally forgot about the arrangement until they were married thirty years later, at which time the allowance stopped. However, Marie Harriman's efforts to remove her husband permanently from Pamela's thrall were apparently quite successful. They didn't see each other again until years later.

James L. Greenfield, the former assistant managing editor of the *New York Times Magazine* and now a member of the editorial board of the *New York Times*, told me a story that proved how effective Marie's ban was in keeping them apart.

When Winston Churchill died in 1965, a special plane of dignitaries, led by former President Eisenhower, was sent to England to attend the funeral. The other passengers were Chief Justice Earl Warren, Dean Rusk, Averell Harriman, Kay Halle and Winston Churchill's butler, who had been on a yacht in Palm Beach.

"I was on the plane traveling with Dean Rusk," recounted Greenfield. Kay Halle was a member of the Halle Brothers department store family who had developed a power base in the Democratic Party and had a strong tie to the Churchills. She was reputed to be the person who had single-handedly convinced the United States government to grant Winston

Churchill the American citizenship to which he was entitled through his American mother, the famous Jenny Jerome. It was a rite Ms. Halle saw as bestowing honor on both Churchill and this country. Kay Halle was also widely reputed to be deeply in love with the highly unlovable Randolph Churchill, which proves that there's always someone for everyone.

"On the return trip from London," Greenfield said, "we picked up some other passengers, Teddy Kennedy and Pamela Churchill. I can recall the scene vividly. Pamela swept on to the plane swathed in full-length mink and immediately spotted Averell. The two of them fell upon each other like long-lost friends, with such delight and enthusiasm that it was apparent they hadn't seen each other for years. I watched them from time to time, and her eyes were just riveted to his face. He had recently returned from Vietnam and was regaling her with details of his trip. She listened with the kind of rapt attention for which she was renowned."

Pamela and Randolph Churchill were divorced at the end of the war, and according to a well-known English author who was a friend of the family, Winston was devastated by the breakup and treated his ex-daughter-in-law very generously, giving her many lovely heirlooms and priceless pieces of antique furniture.

Now we come to Phase II: Pamela in postwar Paris. The French capital was gay, fun and filled with all the Beautiful People. The world's wealthy were making up for the deprivations of the war years and were spending previously paralyzed funds on extravagant parties, entertainments and ostentation. Pamela set herself up in a fancy flat near the Rue President Wilson and created a salon par excellence that was to be her focal point for acquiring a successor to Randolph. Her son was farmed out to various friends, relatives and, later on, schools. Nothing must interfere with the quest for a wealthy important husband.

How she subsidized such high living can only be conjectured—Averell's generous stipend, a small allowance from her father, some Churchill support, possibly a little help from friends and lovers. She was also reputed to have made a few francs by finding paintings for people and then picking up sizable commissions for her efforts. A woman who had been Stavros Niarchos's curator told me how they had acquired a van Dongen through Pamela. She worked so that no stigma of crass trade entered the negotiations. "She phoned and said, 'I've seen the most divine van Dongen! Come to tea and you'll see it.' You'd have a lovely tea with the dealer who was there with the painting, the purchase was made, and Pamela made a tidy bit. It was all quite pleasant and civilized."

Her parties, gift-giving and life-style were lavish, but then you can't catch a rich husband without the proper setting. Elegant furniture, fine linens and china, exquisite porcelains, properly hung paintings, all these are important to create the sort of aura of comfortable luxury in which the extremely rich feel at home. Pamela studied furnishings and furniture and worked with an interior decorator to develop the taste and knowledge required to achieve the subtle ambience of wealth that seems to elude the nouveau riche, who stuff their homes with costly pieces and end up with that expensively over-decorated look that's great for photographing but lousy for living.

Her first major conquest was the very, very rich Italian magnate Gianni Agnelli, whom she wooed with a dedication that went as far as her actually taking on an Italian accent from time to time and converting to Catholicism. Later on, when she became involved with the superrich Elie de Rothschild, she became an expert on Louis Seize furniture. Man-pleasing is Pamela's career and she gives it her total attention. As her friend Leonora Hornblow said in the *Vanity Fair* article, "When Pamela met a man she adored, she just unconsciously assumed his identity as if she were putting on a glove."[4]

But Agnelli did not marry her, nor did Rothschild, nor any of the succession of wealthy lovers who followed, such as Aly Kahn, Stavros Niarchos, Aristotle Onassis and Jock Whitney. By the end of the 1950s, Pamela was forty years old, had gone through most of the powerful men in Europe and was still single. It was becoming an embarrassment. She needed validation, she needed the legitimacy of a husband, or she would end as just another used-up international courtesan with a reputation. On a visit to New York, where she was a guest of William and Babe Paley, she was introduced to Leland Hayward and apparently decided he was the chosen one. It was a wise decision, because her past, which came off as ho-hum tawdry to the European elite, sounded enchantingly alluring to the American Leland Hayward, who was awed to be with the daughter-in-law of Winston Churchill, daughter of a baron, a woman who had slept with half the international jet set.

The details of how Pamela won Leland away from Slim Keith are covered in Slim's chapter, so I'll just take off from the point of her marriage and new position as Mrs. Leland Hayward. As usual, she committed herself to the task of becoming totally immersed in his life and assuming the role of the wife of one of Broadway and Hollywood's leading lights. Within a few weeks of their marriage, she was quoting box-office grosses. When he went on the road for out-of-town tryouts, she was there cooking for him on a hotel hot plate, sitting in on script conferences, sharing his suffering over flops. Of course, how much of this was devotion and how much distrust we'll never know. She knew what had happened when his former wife had let him out of her sight for a month. She set up another of her elegant antique-filled abodes at 1020 Fifth Avenue and proceeded to create a cocoon for Leland the likes of which he had never had. Instead of meeting his pals at the usual celebrity spots, he would go home for lunch, where Pamela had created a paradise geared to providing wraparound pleasure for her man. Maybe a masseur would be there, or a manicurist, or whatever service she felt Leland would enjoy. She cosseted him, she catered to him, she made him feel like the most important man in the world, and he adored her.

Her life as Mrs. Hayward should have been idyllic. How could any man be anything but ecstatic under a regimen of total indulgence? Pamela's technique had always been to create a perfectly controlled environment in which her mate could flourish under her care. She was skilled in this process, but completely unable to deal with the outside forces that must inevitably pierce the protective walls she had artificially constructed. In this case, it was the three Hayward children from his marriage to Margaret Sullavan: Brooke, Bill, and Bridget. They were young, very troubled beings who had already been through the trauma of their father's breaking up their home and divorcing their mother to marry Slim Hawks, whom they had come to accept and then love. Now they were not only going to lose the warm and friendly Slim, but would have to face this cold woman, who did not have a clue about motherhood.

There is a popularly accepted myth that all women have a natural maternal instinct. Just hand any female a baby and instantly she will become a competent, caring mother. Buffalo chips. There are millions of women who wouldn't know which end of the kid to grab and have an aversion to the whole dirty mess. They have no depth of understanding and natural maternal wisdom to tap into in order to guide their children. Unable to depend on their own instincts, such people inevitably resort to rule-making and discipline. As they cannot read children's reactions, they invariably make horrendous gaffes. Pamela Hayward had spent her life developing the skills to be a perfect wife, but had no training in being a perfect mother. Instead of allowing a relationship to develop easily and naturally, she "handled" Leland's children. Dicta were issued regarding whom they should or should not date and who were or were not appropriate companions. With total disregard for her stepdaughter's feelings, concerned only about sparing her husband the unpleasantness, she broke the news to Brooke of her mother's possible suicide and, later, her sister Bridget's. Of course, this cruelty does not absolve Leland, who should have insisted on being the one to bring such information to his own children, rather than relying on a stranger. Her coldness to the children became legendary, and she continually complained to friends about those dreadful Hayward children. But the ultimate act of insensitivity, bordering on the vengeful, was at Leland's funeral; she had her son Winston, and not one of Leland's children, deliver the eulogy. It was the ultimate shutout.

Leland Hayward left half of his estate to his children. Brooke recalled that Pam was furious and actually said to her, "How could I have been married for so many years to a man who would leave me so little?"

A few months after Leland Hayward died, Marie Harriman died and left a grief-stricken, aging widower. For months, Averell seemed so lost and inconsolable that his family became concerned. Then one evening, *Washington Post* publisher Katherine Graham prevailed upon the eighty-year-old Averell to attend a dinner party to which she had invited fifty-one-year-old Pamela Hayward and no one else. Pam and Averell spent the evening reminiscing about the old London days, and soon a relationship developed. In September 1971 they were married, with Ethel Kennedy as their witness. Once more, Pamela moved in and transformed her husband's life into one of total perfection.

In his book, *Billy Baldwin, An Autobiography*, published in 1985 by Little, Brown & Co., the decorator talks about how he and Pamela rearranged Harriman's not overly grand but large Federal house on N Street in Georgetown. Baldwin says Pamela is not only the most perfect hostess, who serves delicious food, but that she has the gift of making a person feel that he or she is the only person in the world with whom she wants to be speaking. What he says about her treatment of Harriman is revealing.

"She treats her husband as though he were a dazzling young boy and she a young girl. In no time at all she changed his entire outlook on life."[5]

"She knows how to make a wonderful home for a man," says James Greenfield, who visited them a number of times. "She creates a background, a comforting setting. There are those antique pieces that Winston Churchill had given her, and the marvelous paintings, of course. She has superb taste," he said admiringly.

As she had done with Leland Hayward's house in Westchester, Pamela redid the Harriman house with her special touch, making the place warm, fresh and elegant. The pillows were refilled with down, the furniture reupholstered, new bright chintzes added and the famous Harriman pictures, including a van Gogh, rehung. She devoted herself to becoming the perfect wife and to making her husband into the best possible Averell Harriman he could be. As she had taken on another religion to please Agnelli, so she took on another nationality to please Harriman, becoming an American citizen. Everybody who saw them or spent time with them noted how she made her husband's life a perfect heaven. But once again, she made his family's life a perfect hell.

The grandchildren, who had been close to Averell, now found they were, as had been the Hayward children, shut off from access and denied the old, easy ways that are an accepted part of most family relationships. No longer could they just drop in; Pamela required appointments. The one most hurt was Peter Duchin, who was brought up by the Harrimans, as his mother had died when he was a baby, and his father, pianist Eddy Duchin, was always away on the road. When his father died, Harriman became Peter's legal guardian.

"There was a real father-son relationship between Averell

and Peter," said James Greenfield. "The Harriman children were rarely around, they were off somewhere pursuing their own lives. But Peter was always there. You could see the love and devotion on both sides."

When Peter heard that Pamela planned to sell the Harriman property in Hobe Sound, Florida, he reminded her that Averell had promised him an acre, on which he intended to build a house. When Pamela learned that this was merely a verbal promise, she refused to honor it. Needless to say, Peter does not feel any great affection for Pamela. However, he at least has the advantage of having a wife with whom he can share his antipathy; Peter Duchin is now married to Brooke Hayward.

Pamela was back in the milieu which she knew so well: politics. It is an arena in which she flourishes and she now found herself the wife of a man who had been adviser to four presidents, ambassador to two countries, as well as governor of New York. But not everyone was impressed with Harriman. President Eisenhower called him a "complete nincompoop." In Henry Fairlie's August 22, 1988, article in *The New Republic* entitled "Shamela," he writes, "Nothing in any meeting with Harriman, and little in the available accounts of his public service, gives one any reason for believing that Eisenhower was being altogether unfair. Harriman was one of those strange Washington figures who effortlessly acquire a reputation for wisdom and cunning. But Washington easily detects wisdom in $75 million."[6] Of course, perhaps all those millions remained intact due to the less than philanthropic bent of the family. It is strange that there are Carnegie libraries, universities and hospitals all over the country; there are Rockefeller foundations and institutes. But for all E. A. Harriman's railroad-acquired millions, the only visible display of generosity is Harriman State Park.

However he achieved it, Averell Harriman was an elder statesman highly respected by many and a major factor in the Democratic party, positions he had let slip as he got older.

Enter Pamela, arise Averell. She reawoke his political interest and began filling the house with politicians and diplo-
mats. She had him buy an estate in nearby Middleburg, Virginia, so that she could indulge her passion for horses, and
also because it was a great place to entertain important people who would gladly take the hour drive to enjoy a weekend or lunch in the lavish Pamela style.

"I believe that Ave deliberately set Pamela up with an
after-career in politics for when he was gone," Jim Greenfield told me. "He gave her large amounts of money to do-
nate to the Democratic party and candidates. He well knew
that contributions give you power and access; politicians
smell money and they're around. He had her arrange soirées
and invited important people so that she would develop a
platform." It was not unusual for him to say at the beginning
of a get-together: "This is really Pam's evening," thus endowing her with his imprimatur so that everyone would
know that she was a serious person to be listened to.

And listen they did. But then, one does tend to pay serious
attention to anyone who commands millions. Soon she had
an office, complete with secretary and public relations people, and Pamela the politico was born.

During the last five years of his life, Averell began to lose
his faculties. But the determined Pamela kept up the public
facade of his undiminished importance. She continued to seat
him at the head of the table and act as though he were aware
and participating in all discussions. She would say, "Yes,
Averell agrees with you," and then turn to him to talk about
the issue under discussion, keeping the pretense that he was
totally compos mentis. This pose suited her public image and
created much admiration for her patience and devotion.
However, a journalist who interviewed them alone in their
home told me how disgusted she was with Pamela's peremp-
tory and almost cruel treatment of her husband. When he
wanted to take the interviewer into the adjacent room to
show her some Churchill memorabilia of which he was obvi-

ously proud, Pamela admonished him coldly to sit down. However, in all fairness, living with a person with severely diminished faculties is torturous, and it is almost impossible to check one's irritation all the time.

Averell Harriman died in 1986 at age ninety-four, and much to his children's shock, everything went to his widow. The figure constantly mentioned is $75 million, and then there are the houses and the fantastic collection of priceless paintings. However, there's no need to be incensed at the pecuniary punishment being imposed upon the children; their millions were set into place years ago. Nor could any-one accuse Pamela of being a gold-digging hussy who took an old man for all she could get. She gave good value; she was a devoted wife for fifteen years and did make his declining years extremely happy.

Pamela Churchill Hayward Harriman is one woman about whom no one would question, "What has *she* got?" She isn't sublimely gorgeous, or scintillatingly brilliant, but she has the prized ability to make a man feel special, the greatest attribute of all courtesans.

"She comes across as giving her full attention to you," said Jim Greenfield. "She listens intently, as though every word you say is important. You sense that she really wants you to feel comfortable." And then he added with a laugh, "You almost think she's about to bring you your slippers."

Today Pamela has reached another pinnacle of power. In 1980 she formed a political fund-raising group called Democrats for the Eighties, initially dubbed "Pam PAC," and has now become a driving political force in her own right. No longer in need of a rich husband from whom to derive power, she is functioning on her own and at age seventy is putting all those managerial skills previously used to acquire men to the new purpose of leading them. As Jim Greenfield said, "Pamela's aphrodisiac is public power." Well, she's got it now. I'd say she deserves it.

References

1. "The Prime of Pamela Harriman," Marie Brenner, *Vanity Fair*, July 1988.
2. *Ibid.*
3. *Ibid.*
4. *Ibid.*
5. *Billy Baldwin, An Autobiography*, New York: Little, Brown & Company, 1985.
6. "Shamela," Henry Fairlie, *New Republic*, August 22, 1988, p. 21.

CHAPTER VII

GLITZY TROPHY WIVES

Susan Gutfreund and
Georgette Mosbacher

*It is a truth universally acknowledged, that a
single man in possession of a good fortune, must be
in want of a wife.*
—Jane Austen,
Pride and Prejudice

IN THE EIGHTIES a new job title emerged for a position that
requires skill, dedication, persistence and concentrated executive search efforts on a par with those conducted by top-
flight headhunters. "Trophy Wife" is the name coined by
Fortune magazine in 1989 to identify the new wave of
younger women (not too young—bimbos need not apply)
whom CEOs and millionaires marry in synergistic rites
whereby she delights him by making his life a hedonistic
playground and he rewards her by allowing her to spend his
millions in de trop Marie Antoinette let-'em-eat-cake style.

This new job category owes its birth to what doomsayers
call the new Sodom-and-Gomorrah morality that presages
Armageddon and what aging sixties flower children call,
with the pride of accomplishment, the new Free Life-style,
which translates into fuck-you-I-got-mine. This new openness
and acceptance of that I-have-only-one-life-to-live philosophy, which grants entitlement to dump guiltlessly anyone
who impedes your pursuit of perfect pleasure, has finally
reached that heretofore unbreachable bastion of conservative

97

Susan and John Gutfreund at the Metropolitan Museum for a Council of Fashion Designers of America gala, January 1988. *(Photo by Robin Platzer Twin Images)*

morality, the executive boardroom. Years ago, an executive's rise through the corporation was dependent upon his stability and rectitude, which precluded the possibility of divorce. A good faithful wife at his side was a vital piece of equipment for the ambitious, and a "fine family man" was the approving epithet applied to every successful corporate achiever. In the eyes of the board of directors, this stainless image conveyed a sense of solidity and dependability to stockholders and customers. A man who did not respect the sacred contract of marriage was not looked upon with favor by *Fortune* 500 companies. After all, who would trust the running of a company to a man who could not control his own home life?

Today a CEO who walks into the annual corporate bash with his gray-haired original wife is regarded with wonder and raised eyebrows. Why is he still wearing a Timex when he can now afford a Rolex? The guy's obviously a square. Or maybe he's one of those old-fashioned honorable types who's not up to the challenges of guiding an organization

Georgette Mosbacher at her desk in the New York office of LaPrairie, May 1989. *(AP/World Wide Photos)*

through the treacherous mine fields of today's volatile markets while fending off the roving slimebucket financiers; in this era we need a ruthless risk-taker at the top.

The new morality of the boardroom has drawn a group of shrewd opportunists—women to whom this trend is the equivalent of Sutter's gold strike. In some ways, they're not unlike the guys who suddenly materialized like a cloud of gnats during the housing boom to hustle storm windows and aluminum siding, then moved into hawking solar heating and attic insulation when energy conservation became the rage, and are now out there pushing car phones. These women have spotted the ripe possibilities presented by the new corporate acceptance of spouse-shedding and are out there on intense reconnaissance missions among the growing supply of vulnerable, aging tycoons.

It's been an absolute boon to women who years ago would have been classified as over the hill and unmarketable. Think of it. What do you do if you are a good-looking woman of

Georgette Mosbacher with husband Secretary of Commerce Robert Mosbacher at pre-inaugural gala, January 18, 1989. *(AP/World Wide Photos)*

thirty or more who craves wealth that you now know you will never be able to earn yourself? Forty-two-year-old guys don't want you, they're out there trolling for twenty-year-olds. But by whom are you viewed as desirable and deliciously young? Fifty-, sixty- and seventy-year-olds, the ones who have already made their millions, so that you can fall right into their pots of gold without having to pay the dues of struggling together through the upward-drive travails. The new boardroom mentality that freed top execs to divorce without causing stock-shaking scandals has produced a vast, glittering supply of suddenly eligible men who are being picked off by this new class of predatory women who are looking for a quick and easy road to riches.

It's not hard to lure him away from his wife of forty years. He put many tough years into building his success while the little woman ran his home and raised the children. Now he's ready to relax and enjoy the fruits of his labors, to revel in his achievements and hard-won status. He would like to be treated at home with the deference he gets at the office and the gratitude to which he feels he's entitled for having provided the family with a big house, sports cars for the sixteen-year-old, ski and sun vacations, designer jeans and college educations free of the onus of student loans. Instead, he's taken for granted by a jaded helpmeet who knew him when, and criticized by sulky children whose expensive shrinks encourage them to blame their irresponsibilities and failures on dad's workaholic neglect. The guy's a prime candidate for an unfriendly takeover—and there's a whole new tribe of women out there who are looking for just such pigeons.

There are very specific job requirements for the position as Trophy Wife. (1) You can't be too young, since that would make the elderly groom look like an undignified, cradle-robbing asshole. Also, you must have the maturity and experience to know exactly where to throw away his money in order to get the biggest bang for his buck. (2) Appearance is everything. Crow's feet, sagging breasts and droopy tushes are definite no-no's; he had that already. Stylish and stunning is a must, which means vigilant visits to the hairdresser and cosmetic surgeon. Stringent dieting, personal trainers and frequent liposuctions are part of your regular program. (3) You must know how to extol his virtues publicly and convincingly so that he actually believes he is adorable and that you love him and not his money. (4) Creativity and competence are needed to handle the needs of the faltering libido and sometimes dysfunctional equipment of the aging male and one must be cheerfully willing to administer blow jobs on call. After all, what are you there for if not to help him live out his wildest fantasies?

As you can see, becoming a Trophy Wife is rarely the result of casual conquest; it takes tenacity and long-term planning. The technique is to work your way up to the big payoff by starting on the matrimonial cavalcade with a smaller fish or two, maybe a local millionaire here and there, while always being on the alert for the big shark; keeping your guy reasonably happy at home but being ever vigilant on the outside. Marriage is not an institution, merely an incentive, and the till-death-do-us-part oath is as meaningful as the signature on your income tax return that attests to the validity of all the figures therein. It's the first catch that's the hardest, because once she sees, as her mother said, that it's just as easy to fall for a rich man as a poor one and to get him to fall for her, then how do you keep 'em down on the farm?

Two leading ladies of this new Trophy Wife breed are Susan Gutfreund and Georgette Mosbacher. While neither one was endowed by nature with striking beauty or startling brilliance, both were born with driving desires to be prominent and profligate.

Susan Gutfreund is a former airline stewardess who, at age thirty-two, married fifty-two-year-old John Gutfreund, billionaire CEO of Salomon, Inc., the investment banking firm made infamous in Michael Lewis's Wall Street-bashing bestseller, *Liar's Poker*.

"The leading indicator of the shift in the collective personality of our firm was the social life of our chairman and CEO, John Gutfreund. He had married a woman with burning social ambition twenty years his junior. She threw parties and invited gossip columnists. Her invitations, the value of which seemed to rise and fall with our share price, were wrapped in a tiny bow and delivered by hand. She employed a consultant to ensure she and her husband received the right sort of coverage. And though she did not go so far as to insist that the employees of Salomon Brothers were made as presentable as her husband (whom she stuffed into a new wardrobe), it was impossible in our company for some of this indulgence and posturing not to trickle down."[1]

Susan Kaposta Penn Gutfreund (she insists on the anglicized pronunciation "Goodfriend") claims she loves cool houses because it takes her back to her childhood in the fifteenth-century thatched-roof house in which she was born in England. Her father, Louis, a man who served thirty years in the air force, cannot account for her preference for low temperatures, as the home where she was born in Chicago was always comfortably heated. If she is attempting to imply a British lineage, it would be difficult to explain the name "Kaposta," which is the Russian word for sauerkraut. Any claims she may make for having had a well-traveled background can be accepted, as a father in the air force means constant shifting and, according to her mother, who is of Spanish descent and named America, Susan grew up "all over the place." And then there was the frequent-flier mileage she logged as an airline stewardess, which is how she met her first husband.

Susan's first marriage was to John Roby Penn of Fort Worth, heir to a real estate fortune. The marriage lasted from 1970 to 1975, when they divorced. Penn has married several times since. After the divorce, Susan hung around Fort Worth for a while and, according to Cissy Stewart, former society reporter of the *Fort Worth Telegram*, "was out to catch a rich husband." But the pickings were lean, so she headed north, ran into silver-haired John Gutfreund, and knew at once that her eagle had landed. In these campaigns of marital blitz one never leaves anything to chance. Susan checked out all possible connections. She knew Sandy Lowenstein, whose husband, Huey, was an investment banker at Donaldson, Lufkin & Jenrette and a friend of Gutfreund's. She asked Sandy to arrange a dinner with John, which she did, and the rest is history.

John Gutfreund has thick lips, wears glasses and is pudgy and short, although as the old joke goes, when he stands on his money he's very tall. When they met, Susan was in her thirties and John in his fifties. As he's not a Mel Gibson lookalike, we must assume Susan saw past the unimposing appearance and was attracted by other attributes. Legend has it that John and Susan were so taken with each other at that first meeting they almost had to be torn apart at the close of the evening. Obviously love at first sight. And apparently Susan's parents liked him. According to *New York* magazine,

America Kaposta thought John was super. "If he were a plumber, a bus driver, an electrician, it wouldn't matter," said she, obviously without consulting her daughter. "He himself is such a wholesome, humble, wonderful son-in-law."[2] Obviously, perceptions differ, because "humble" and "wholesome" are not words readily associated with the man who was fast developing a reputation on Wall Street for ruthlessness.

Susan and John were married in 1981, and she embarked upon a campaign to become the leading social figure in New York and Paris and to make the heretofore staid, paunchy John Gutfreund into an urbane sophisticate on two continents, no matter what it cost.

Years ago, New York society was formed by robber barons and master swindlers with names such as Astor, Harriman, Morgan, Vanderbilt and Rockefeller (no Jews or Catholics need apply). As the generations changed, the names stayed the same but the tone of society's public behavior became one of elegant restraint, as behooved expensively educated men and women who grew up with wealth and were taught the importance of a social conscience. The *New York Times* had a society page in which were dutifully reported the social doings of doyennes with old-money names. Today there is no longer a society page; it's called the Family Page. And it is filled with the antics of Trophy Wife arrivistes who have attempted to create their own high society with the old-line focus of good works and charity balls, to which this new group has added their own accent of excrescent, flashy flamboyance.

In social events, there is usually a discernible ratio of splash to security, the longer-standing the affluence of the hosts, the less elaborate the affair. If you attend a four-alarm wedding where the hors d'oeuvre table stretches twenty feet across and is manned by four white-toqued chefs skillfully carving filets and broiling baby lamb chops, followed by a six-course meal complete with vintage wines, topped off by a caloric obscenity called a Viennese Table, and the wedding processional is accompanied by the New York Philharmonic with Madonna singing "Because," you know the father of the bride is a neo-millionaire who four years ago was wearing iridescent raincoats and Thom McAn shoes. When you are invited to a similar occasion given by Old Money, eat before you leave home.

People who are accustomed to affluence are secure in the knowledge that everyone knows of their wealth and they have no reason to put on a show. In fact, it is regarded as poor taste. But the schnooks who just made it feel you have to see it to believe it.

Susan Gutfreund spends money like a typist who just won the lottery. She had a refrigerator placed in her bathroom because she likes her after-bath perfumes chilled. Her parties are legendary for their excesses and it is believed that Tom Wolfe modeled the nouveau-riche couple in *The Bonfire of the Vanities* after the Gutfreunds. Invitations are not only delivered by hand by their chauffeur, but each arrives pinned with a yellow rose. Presents are sent the same way, usually in monogrammed shopping bags topped with monogrammed black and white ribbons. She had their huge two-floor apartment in River House extensively and expensively restructured and redecorated in an ambivalent olio of stark modernity and eighteenth-century France, featuring a dramatic swirling staircase and a Robert Adam carpet. She hired society decorators Chessy Rayner and Mica Ertegun, who gutted the four-bedroom apartment and converted it into a one-bedroom flat. Fully half of the second floor was converted into a vast bathroom and dressing room with closet space for a cast of thousands. Obviously, Susan was planning to acquire a wardrobe to suit her new grand life-style. Just three years later, the Gutfreunds were becoming crowded, what with six servants and a baby son. So in 1985 they moved to a large Fifth Avenue apartment and, as befitting a woman who has enjoyed tremendous wealth for all of four years, Susan spent an estimated $20 million under the guidance of the French decorator Henri Samuel to create a suitably Old Money environment. The apartment is filled with instant heirlooms and priceless French antiques so that Susan can now enjoy the cachet of being a collector. When anyone admires a piece, she replies with the offhand air of the heiress, "Thank you, I've had it for ages."

Not content to make a name in New York so-called society, Susan Gutfreund decided to expand her social horizons across the ocean by acquiring a Paris flat in a house on the Rue de Grenelle and building another temple of excess. She did not like the idea of leaving the cars out in the courtyard overnight, exposed to the nasty *neige* and *pluie.* So for a mere million dollars she had an underground garage constructed that has been described as looking like a ballroom, which means the Gutfreund cars are now housed in better quarters than half the Parisians. Madame Defarge, where are you when we need you? While Henri Samuel was redoing the mansion in the style to which Susan was now totally accustomed, she, her young son John Peter and his nanny stayed for months on end in a $1,000-a-day suite at the Ritz. Besides pouring money into the house, she poured *beaucoup de francs* into French causes, which bought her passage into French *société* and brought her into the orbit of such people as the Baroness Marie-Helene de Rothschild. How's that for a social coup for little Susie Kaposta?

In an article about the Gutfreunds that appeared in the January 10, 1988, issue of the *New York Times Magazine*, the publicist Eleanor Lambert is quoted as saying, "Susan's wanted to make the big time and she's done it better than anyone I know. . . . She's right from Trollope and Wharton . . . she's her own invention."[3] She is also one of those people who is impossible to caricature, as she is naturally a caricature, even to the point of mouthing such Marie Antoinette epigrams as "It's so expensive to be rich."

In the same article, the designer Bill Blass, who, I would

assume from the diplomatic description that follows, must enjoy a good bit of Mrs. Gutfreund's custom, says, "Susan's bright and she's developed a personal style all for herself."

Actually, her style is not all that personal but rather resembles one commonly known as "Early Social Climber," which has cropped up on the American scene with dismal regularity throughout our history. All it takes is serious money, powerful ambition and an indulgent spouse.

That brings us to Mr. Gutfreund. You might wonder how a tough self-made millionaire dubbed by *Business Week* the King of Wall Street could allow himself to become a pussycat in the hands of an ex-stewardess who is striving mightily to turn him into a social lion and herself into Susan the Queen of the Jungle. John Gutfreund is the all-powerful CEO of Salomon, Inc., an international investment bank with three billion dollars in capital and employing six thousand people worldwide in 1987. Mr. Gutfreund made himself $40 million on the sale of Salomon Brothers in 1981. Besides the income generated by this little windfall, there is always his annual salary of $3.1 million to keep the home fires burning.

John Gutfreund grew up in Scarsdale, New York, in a well-to-do-family that belonged to the Century Country Club in Purchase, at that time a social center for the German Jewish establishment. John graduated from Oberlin College and intended to teach literature but took a job in the meantime in the Wall Street bond house of Salomon Brothers & Hutzler through the introduction his father arranged with fellow club member, William "Billy" Salomon. John joined the firm as a $24-a-week trainee in the statistics department and, showing a real talent for trading, moved swiftly up through the ranks to become a partner at thirty-four. In the late 1950s, he met and married Joyce Low, a member of the wealthy Low family, which was an upward step for John. Her father, Teddy Low, was a partner at Bear, Stearns & Company. They moved into a nice apartment on Lexington Avenue and Joyce performed the prescribed wifely role expected of members

of assimilated German Jewish families who are obsessively
understated and low-key, so as never to be confused with
those loud and boisterous Eastern European Jews. She
dressed simply, raised their three sons and became involved
in good works while John put in long hours at the office and
developed a reputation for aggressiveness and imagination.
When Billy Salomon stepped down in 1978, he appointed
John Gutfreund as his successor. At that time the firm was a
privately held partnership. About four years later, without
bothering to discuss it with or even tell Billy Salomon of his
intentions, Gutfreund sold the firm for $554 million to Phil-
bro, the publicly held commodities company. Though Billy
had essentially created the firm, he ended up with a not-too-
shabby $10 million from the sale, but Gutfreund walked
away with close to $40 million. Now king of the hill, Gut-
freund got to work on David Tendler, the head of Philbro,
who, under the terms of the merger, was to be the chief
executive of the newly formed Philbro-Salomon, while Gutfreund was to run Salomon Brothers as a smaller independent division.

Came the recession of the early 1980s and the commodities market was wounded, while the stock market rally sent
Salomon's profits zooming. This offered Gutfreund the opportunity to persuade the joint companies' board to name
him "co-chief executive," which put Tendler on tenterhooks
and sent him into secret negotiations to buy back his commodities operation. The deal collapsed when word leaked
out, which enabled an indignant Gutfreund to demand that
he replace the treacherous Tendler, to which the board
readily agreed. Now the reigning monarch of Philbro-Salomon, Gutfreund proceeded to sell off Philbro's operations,
cut its personnel by two-thirds and then in 1985, to purge all
traces of Philbro by changing the name of the company to
Salomon, Inc. The wholesome, humble son-in-law had van-
quished his enemies and was now conqueror-in-chief of all
he surveyed.

It's tough work making millions. A man needs distraction, a respite from the wars. The Roman emperors came home to wild orgies, John comes home to Susan and her extravaganzas. Back in the days of his first marriage, he lived the life of a sober, responsible family man and probably came home to a quiet dinner in an apartment furnished in the usual drab elegance of the era. Today he comes home to opulence and excesses and lavish dinners such as the one Susan threw for Henry Kissinger's sixtieth birthday (with a guest list ranging from Stavros Niarchos to the then-Mrs. Johnny Carson), at which Susan's chef created a sensation with a dessert of green apples made of spun sugar, using a technique he had learned from the glassblowers of Murano. John is having one hell of a good time. As he told a reporter in 1984, "Susan has enriched my life," and has certainly unenriched his bank account, but he doesn't seem to care.

Susan makes him happy. She makes him feel loved. She makes him feel vital. She takes charge of his life after five (millionaires don't stay late at the office—that went out with the first wife), and she has brought him into an exciting social whirl he never before enjoyed. Opera galas, museum benefits, charity balls—it's just one gay round of glittering festivities at which he is heartily welcomed as moola con grata. He has spent his life making money, and now she's showing him how to enjoy life by spending it. He finds himself rubbing tuxedoed elbows with movie stars, talking with famous artists and writers, even dining with people named Astor and Vanderbilt who would never have permitted him a glass of water at their clubs. It's positively heady, a fantasy-land he never had dreamed of entering. And at his side or dancing in his arms is adoring Susan, always at the ready to grant his slightest whim. She's young (by his mature standards), she's pretty, she's a shiksa. She is the bird of paradise who has brought him into this wondrous fun world where life is indeed a cabaret. He was over fifty when they met, maybe starting to think he was good for nothing more than fading off into old farthood and, instead, she has remade him into an active, sophisticated bon vivant. So maybe it is a tad superficial, this sybaritic night-after-night dancing among beautiful designer-dressed women displaying yards of surgically smoothened skin, exchanging animated banalities for the roving camera, and treating him like royalty just because he bankrolled the affair. So what if Susan is spending his millions like there's no tomorrow? Maybe there isn't. Besides, as long as she's spending income and not capital, who cares? Right now, the little woman is working hard to keep him happily fulfilled on all levels, and maybe on some he never knew existed. From John Gutfreund's point of view, he is getting full quid for his quo.

Georgette Mosbacher is a different type but with similar goals. She comes to the job of Trophy Wife with excellent references: first husband, real-estate-rich Robert Muir (1970, Los Angeles); second husband, Fabergé-rich George Barrie (1980, New York); third husband—the jackpot—$200-million-oil-rich Robert Mosbacher (1985, Houston).

If you think any of these big-bucks matrimonial acquisitions came about by chance, you haven't met Georgette. This curvaceous redhead has always known what she wanted—big money—and has worked conscientiously to get it.

When I phoned Georgette Mosbacher's New York office —oh yes, she works, but more about that later—I was given the phone number of the public relations person who handles all Ms. Mosbacher's contacts with the press. This turned out to be an Indiana area code, which is Georgette's home state, and the public relations woman named Lyn Gastevich turned out to be Georgette's sister and a very nice lady who sounded as if she spends a lot of time transmitting opinions and conclusions in which she has been permitted no input. First, she advised me that her sister had to see a projected list of questions before she might consider allowing me to interview her. Why not? The queen of England has the same stipulation. Then she informed me, in a voice that carried the level of conviction of someone passing on a message with which she is not totally in accord, that Ms. Mosbacher did not wish to be interviewed because both of her ex-husbands were still alive. That reminded me of a joke about a ninety-year-old couple who wanted a divorce. When the attorney asked why they took twenty years to decide to break up, they answered, "We were waiting for the kids to die."

Why Ms. Mosbacher finds the presence of live ex-spouses a deterrent to an interview I never learned. I can only conclude that she never speaks ill of the living, only the dead, or that she is loathe to rouse these two heretofore silent gentlemen for fear of stirring up stuff about the early Georgette that the current Ms. Mosbacher would like to keep buried.

Georgette Mosbacher was born in 1948 to working-class parents in Highland, Indiana, a small town twenty-five miles south of Chicago. Her father managed a bowling alley and was killed in an automobile accident when Georgette was seven years old. She was the oldest of four children and was raised by her mother and grandmother. Her mother was a hotel clerk and later worked in a travel agency. She claims that her grandmother was a switchman on the railroad; when the train came, she would pump the switch up and down. In the in-depth interview she gave to John Davidson that appeared in the February 1989 issue of *Vanity Fair*, she tells about a grandfather who was killed collecting rent from a tenant and a grandmother who took his place on the assembly line the very next day. If we can get the cast of characters right here, Georgette had a father and grandfather who died violently and two grandmothers working in rather unusual and strenuous jobs. No matter how accurate the details, it certainly sounds as though Georgette did not grow up in an Ozzie-and-Harriet home. Such a background either pulls you down into repeat poverty, or drives you to ambitious self-improvement. Her sister recalls that Georgette played with make-believe plastic jewelry, which she called "diamonds" and "pearls," and always craved a caviar life far above the mean streets of Indiana.

She attended Indiana University in the sixties but the free-wheeling, explosive college campus activities of the anti-Vietnam era passed her by because she had to work two jobs, as a switchboard operator and billing clerk, in order to put herself through school. Upon graduation, she taught for a semester and then went to Los Angeles, where her brother was in school. She got a job with an advertising agency and then formed a small company to produce commercials for real estate firms. In 1970 at age twenty-three, she married Robert Muir, a wealthy older Los Angeles real estate developer. ("All my husbands have been successful. All my husbands have been older," she said in an interview.[4]) They divorced in 1977, and one would assume that California's community-property law left her in fair financial shape.

Her next job was as an executive producer in the West Coast office of Fabergé cosmetics in their newly created film production division called Brut Productions. When Ted Turner bought out the division, Georgette moved to the New York offices of Fabergé in the licensing department, where she was involved in marketing and project development. Somehow she managed to meet the sixty-seven-year-old chairman of the company, George Barrie. This was the savvy gentleman who had the foresight to hire Cary Grant as a Fabergé rep. A real promoter, Barrie made friends with stars by giving them lifts across the country in his private jet in the days when personal aircraft were a rarity. Thirty-two-year-old red-haired Georgette was smart, attractive and ambitious, with a body that might not have fit in with fashion editors' anorexic concept of beauty but which certainly fit into an aging male's fantasy. She and Barrie married in 1980 and were divorced two years later. Georgette's learning process was then over; she had completed her apprenticeship and with two wealthy husbands under her belt, so to speak, was now fully trained in the art of finding and marrying a millionaire.

As an experienced businesswoman, she knew how to go about locating a supply of suitable merchandise. The first step is always to find the market where such products abound. That was easy—everyone watching *Dallas* knows that Texas is positively crawling with oil-rich tycoons. When she saw an article in *Texas Monthly* (to which every rich-husband seeker subscribes and probably deducts as a business expense) that mentioned millionaire Robert Mosbacher as the second most eligible man in the world next to Prince Rainier, Georgette headed for Houston. Of course, Texans tend to be rather parochial in their views of life. To declare a Houston oilman the second most eligible man in the entire world may not have been the result of genuine in-depth research, but the conclusion was good enough for Georgette. The determined redhead kept after everyone she knew who might know Mosbacher and called in all her chits until she finally engineered a meeting with the unsuspecting prey.

Robert Mosbacher grew up on Park Avenue and in White Plains, New York, located in high-income Westchester County. His father, Emil Mosbacher, who started out as a runner on the Curb Exchange, made a million dollars by the time he was twenty-one and eventually owned a seat on the American Stock Exchange. The family belonged to the Beach Point Club on Long Island Sound in Mamaroneck, a place founded by wealthy German-Jewish families who restricted membership to exclude those of Eastern European heritage. I knew one of the founders of the club well enough to ask why a refined individual of Russian-Jewish extraction would not be welcomed as a member. He answered in a semi-jocular tone that they feared the possibility that such a person might see fit to invite some of his uncouth relatives, who could conceivably sit around in their underwear. Beach Point had, and still has, one of the finest marinas in the area, and both Robert and his brother Emil, Jr., who was known as

Bus, became fine sailors. Bus Mosbacher, who was chief of protocol under President Richard Nixon, won the America's Cup in 1962 and 1967, and Robert Mosbacher won world championships in two different Olympic classes in 1969 and 1971.

Following a path similar to that of his friend, George Bush, Robert decided to seek his fortune in oil-rich Texas and left the civilized elite of the East for the rough-and-tumble financial world of Houston. Of course, he didn't arrive looking for a handout, but came with $500,000 start-up money from his father.

He was then twenty-one years old, a recent graduate of Washington and Lee, and had a pregnant wife, Jane. He did his daddy proud and developed a reputation as a smart and trustworthy trader. In 1983, his holdings were estimated at about $150 million. He also made quite a reputation as a fund-raiser for the Republican party. He raised $14 million for Gerald Ford in 1976 and $60 million for Bush's successful presidential campaign. Along with James Baker, he is credited with having convinced Bush to withdraw early from the 1980 presidential primaries in order to position himself strategically as a choice for Reagan's vice president.

Jane died of leukemia, and Robert was briefly married to Sandra Gerry of an oil-connected family, among the founders of Humble Oil.

When Georgette embarked on her campaign to catch her third and richest husband, Mosbacher was in his late fifties. Albeit fit and trim with rugged features, blue eyes and an engaging smile, he had to be intensely flattered to be pursued relentlessly by this voluptuous, vivacious thirty-four-year-old redhead who would do absolutely anything to please and procure him in marriage. Let us not forget that she could tap her rich lode of knowledge and experience in the emotional, egotistical and sexual needs of men who have passed their prime. Robert may or may not have been a hot number, but it is a clinical fact that even the most virile of males in their fifties and up do not snap to like they used to, and only a woman who cares a lot is willing to put in the time and effort sometimes needed to keep action going to a satisfactory conclusion. And Georgette cared a lot. After his previous marriage had failed, Robert had vowed never to marry again. But he hadn't met Georgette. As she herself stated, it took her two years of concentrated nonstop effort to win him. She tells the story of Robert singing her the Frank Sinatra song about an irresistible force meeting an immovable object on the night he realized he was going to marry her.

In March 1985, thirty-six-year-old twice-married Georgette became the wife of sixty-year-old Robert Mosbacher, who was then reputed to be worth $200 million. It is not for nothing that the *Washington Post* has dubbed her "The Happy Hoosier."

Marriage to Mosbacher not only brought Georgette access to tremendous wealth, it also catapulted her into the elite levels of Washington. Financial chairman for George Bush's presidential campaign, Robert Mosbacher was rewarded with the position of Secretary of Commerce in 1989, which gives Georgette the added social luster of the position of cabinet wife.

The Nation's February 20, 1989, issue had a special article that asked the question, "Why is Washington gaga over Georgette Mosbacher?" The answer came a few lines later in a quote from the *Washington Post* alerting readers to her "ample cleavage" and the fact that she "filled out her angora sweater" and was "sexy." It also quoted a friend who observed that Georgette and Robert had a "sexual marriage."[5]

In the infamous New York Nouvelle Social Register that evaluates entrants by per-month pictures in *W* and husbands' megabuck donations, Georgette's national status has undoubtedly caused much capped-teeth-gnashing in the boudoirs of Ivana and Susan.

She also gets high rating points in the sumptuous abode category, an absolute must if you wish to be even considered for the title of Mrs.-Millionaire-of-the-Month. Georgette's Sutton Place apartment was featured in one of the glossy, upscale snob shelter magazines that is viewed as another validating coup for the upwardly mobile.

The article, written in the magazine's usual fawn-and-gush-school-of-journalism style, swoons over the overstuffed, baseball field-size living room. Georgette describes the furnishings and decor as being a reflection of her. Are they ever.

A wall of the master bedroom is virtually covered with Scavullo's photograph of Georgette silk-screened nine times, and the living-room fireplace is dominated by a large Aaron Shikler charcoal of Georgette. But the dining room is the *pièce de résistance*, boasting a cerulean blue celestial fantasy ceiling that is a trompe-l'oeil vision of the heavens as seen through the eyes of a poor little girl who grew up to be Queen Midas. It has stars, a shooting comet, the Big Dipper, the Little Dipper, the planets and symbols of the zodiac, all painted in gold.

Georgette seems to be drawn to the skies, as her private office also boasts clouds on the ceiling. Or maybe her painter is like Eldin on *Murphy Brown* and just bought an oversupply of sky blue and cloud white paint.

We also learn that like Noah, Georgette has a penchant for pairs. The place abounds in two of everything. Her bed is flanked by matching George III secretary-bookcases. The living room has two sofas. Georgette must like the symmetry presented by pairs, or possibly the message of bottomless pockets.

The article mentions that when she brings work home, she does it at her bedside desk, which brings us to the new entrepreneur role in her life. In 1988 the Mosbachers came up with $35 million to buy her La Prairie, a company marketing some of America's most expensive skin-care products (a jar of La Prairie eye cream goes for $65), thereby launching Georgette into an orbit parallel to Estée Lauder's and into a new arena that gets her headlined in *Savvy* and *Business Week*.

Now the CEO of a $60-million company, Georgette has moved into the next rank of Trophy Wife status, that of the Working Rich and She Who Must Be Taken Seriously.

It is the "in" trend, and the Trophy Wife who wants to prove that she's not just another pretty face gets hubby to buy her a business. What else? I mean, how many apartments can you furnish, how many baubles can you buy? So big daddy indulges her little whim to the tune of however many millions it takes and she's off and running in the new role of CEO. Carolyne Roehm got leveraged-buyout-specialist husband Henry Kravis to bankroll her fashion company and now Georgette has joined the ranks of glamorous entrepreneurs. La Prairie is a natural choice for her, as it fits in with her background: she was once married to the chairman of a cosmetics company, now she is one herself. She sits in her elegantly decorated Madison Avenue office making important decisions, such as what kind of dresses should be worn by La Prairie saleswomen, and where to get her nails manicured and from which pretzel vendor to buy her Pritikin-diet lunch. She is very busy sending off thank-you notes and RSVPs to invitations, dispatching gifts from Tiffany's and arranging fittings with her dressmaker. It's a bitch.

This is not to say she is not a hard-working executive. She claims to be in the office every morning before eight, a story which is difficult to reconcile with all those photos of her dancing with husband Bob at Washington functions. There is no doubt that La Prairie is an embryonic company that could double its business if managed properly. According to consultants in the cosmetics industry, this would take skillful handling. Whereas most cosmetics firms divide sales among skin care, coloring and fragrance products and thus have three areas for growth potential, La Prairie has limited itself to skin care alone. However, the luxury-priced product line has achieved penetration in such high-end markets as Saks, I. Magnin and Neiman-Marcus stores, which are certainly the right arenas. Although Georgette has hired all the right peo-

ple to run the company, there are rumbles about how difficult she is to work for and with, and how she seems more
interested in using La Prairie to promote herself than the
product line. She admires Estée Lauder to the point of awe
and seems to have set her up as a role model, but Lauder
started her company in order to support her family, and her
success was based on need rather than ego. Motivation
makes a huge difference in building a business.

According to movie producer Allan Carr, an old friend
quoted in the *Vanity Fair* interview, Georgette is "more fascinating and more mysterious than anything Jackie Collins and
Judith Krantz ever dreamed up. She's Lorelei Lee or Stella
Dallas with a happy ending."[6]

I fail to see the mystery in Georgette Mosbacher. She is an
open book that might have been written by Judith Krantz.
She is filled with an obsessive greed for the power of promi-
nence and money, and it is that ambition which drives her.
She has her own funhouse mirror, in which she sees the
many faces of Georgette, and she wants to be them all—
millionaire's wife, head of a multimillion-dollar company,
queen of New York's nouvelle society.

She claims she is seriously concerned with building her
business, and yet spends an enormous amount of office time
on social activities involved in building her socialite image.
She complains that she does not get the credit for working so
hard and points out that men who run companies during the
day and occasionally go out at night are not criticized as she
is. However, a businessman trying to build a company passes
up Bill Blass fashion shows that infringe on business hours.

With Georgette Mosbacher, it's easy to answer the question, "What has SHE got?" A *Texas Monthly* article refers to
her as a "part Damon Runyon broad."[7] In appearance, she is
right out of the page of Fielding's *Tom Jones* and would have
been perfectly cast in the role of the lusty, buxom barmaid
whom all the men adore. Ferociously ambitious and determined, she has an innate chutzpah that makes her impervious

to rejection and impossible to discourage. She is perfectly willing to use her natural attributes plus whatever more it takes to get exactly what she wants.

Being a Trophy Wife is a job that requires the kind of compromises not every woman is willing to make. It sounds like an easy trade-off—she playacts and he pays—but it really isn't. All marriages must be nurtured, but usually it is a joint effort, a shared partnership. Being a Trophy Wife means unilateral giving—she must give him a life of sheer, unadulterated pleasure, vigilantly keep check on his happiness and be attentive and loving at all times. Sure, there's give and take —she gives him fun and joy and he takes it. He gives her lots of money and she takes it. There should be communication in a marriage, but in these relationships, that consists of her asking, "How was your day, honey?" and then doing whatever it takes to make it good.

There are sacrifices to be made. In most cases, the Trophy Wife forgoes motherhood, as children detract from the full-time attention a millionaire husband demands. You cannot relax and grow old gracefully. The signs of age must be eradicated instantly, because they can threaten your position. However, you have to turn a blind eye to his growing gut, disappearing butt and sprouting eyebrows; you must constantly fight to preserve your youth, but pretend to ignore his age. You work twenty-four-hours a day to keep him happy and to keep him from knowing that there is anything in your marriage that isn't absolutely glorious. Does that sound like a drag or what? The plus side is you get to spend millions of dollars with wild abandon and never again have to shop at Loehmann's. Being a Trophy Wife means you never have to say you're sorry, the check is in the mail.

The option is yours. If you're an attractive woman in your thirties looking for a good job, have you considered becoming a Trophy Wife? The pay is good, the benefits fantastic, but the hours are horrendous. If you're qualified and ready, don't mail your résumé: deliver it by hand.

References

1. Michael Lewis, *Liar's Poker*, New York: W. W. Norton & Company, Inc., 1989, p. 48.
2. "Hard to be Rich," John Taylor, *New York*, January 11, 1988, p. 22.
3. "Susan Gutfreund: High Finances, High Living," Carol Vogel, *New York Times Magazine*, January 10, 1988, p. 21.
4. "Where's Georgette?," John Davidson, *Vanity Fair*, February 1989, p. 143.
5. "Manhattan on the Potomac" (Beltway Bandits column), David Corn and Jefferson Morley, *Nation*, February 20, 1989, p. 224.
6. Davidson, *op. cit.*
7. "Zoom at the Top," Mimi Swartz, *Texas Monthly*, December 1988, p. 120.

CHAPTER VIII

GAYFRYD STEINBERG

How to Marry a Billionaire

Man has his will, but woman has her way.
—Oliver Wendell Holmes,
The Autocrat of the Breakfast-Table

THE USUAL SAYING IS, "You are what you eat." But it seems to me, after investigating the fantastic marital successes of the women in this book, that the real adage should be, "You are WHERE you eat." Fateful initial meetings with future husbands always seem to take place at dinner parties where, at some point in the evening, the eminently eligible male suddenly turns to his right, or left, and is struck by a bolt of desire for the stunning, or pretty, or charming (depending on who is telling the story) woman next to him and then, like the epiphany in Jane Austen's *Emma*, "It dart[s] through [him] with the speed of an arrow, that [she] should marry no one but [himself]."

Now I'm as romantic as the next person, but considering that our subjects here are all well past the age of puppy love, the concept of love at first sight would seem implausible. And as all of them have enjoyed a succession of prior spouses and amours, and current morality permits casual sex, it hardly seems possible that they are suffering from the kind of sexual deprivation that would send them into quivering passion at the sight of a particularly juicy décolletage. So there must be more to it than that.

There is. You must be part of the "in" circle so that when

121

Gayfryd and Saul Steinberg at a Metropolitan Museum costume gala, 1988. *(Photo by Robin Platzer Twin Images)*

Gayfryd and Saul Steinberg, at Literacy Volunteers Hoedown, November 1989. *(Photo by Robin Platzer Twin Images)*

these power men meet you, they are secure and comfortable knowing that you have already passed muster and have achieved Top Clearance. It's like the *Good Housekeeping* Seal of Approval: the fact that you are an invited guest to one of the "in" homes assures them that you are a suitable, safe quarry to pursue.

If you want to marry a billionaire, you first want to meet and eat with one on his turf. It is not likely that you will run into a Saul Steinberg at a luncheonette in Brooklyn, although you might have forty years ago, as that is where he spent his childhood. If you are on a quest for a superrich spouse, you introduce yourself into the right society so that you are invited to the kinds of homes that entertain the guys with the big bucks. In the old days when society was spelled with a capital "S," the only acceptable credentials were family. If you carried a 400 Family name, you were regarded as a peer, and the fact that you were a poor relation was of no import. You had to have attended the right schools such as Miss Porter's or Miss Chapin's. You took dance classes at Miss Shippen's. You had a coming-out party, your family attended the designated churches, you summered in Newport, and wintered in Palm Beach. To mingle with the wealthy you needed a blueblood rap sheet.

Today, the only background check they make is at the bank. Susan Penn met John Gutfreund at a dinner party to which she was invited by the wife of an investment banker friend. Gayfryd Johnson met Saul Steinberg at a dinner party at the home of her friend Richard Feigen, the art dealer. In all the interviews with these women, the story always starts from there; no one seems to want to talk about how they, ordinary people with no outstanding credentials such as money, talent, major achievement or striking beauty, developed friendships with the likes of the hosts of these star-studded dinner parties. Susan Penn and Georgette Barrie both professed that their goal-of-the-moment was to snare a rich husband. It would be natural for them to inveigle their way into the society of people who socialize with such men. But Gayfryd Johnson has never indicated that she was one of those predatory females who was out there on the make for a millionaire. However, all three of these women had previously been married to millionaires, which means they were all card-carrying members of the elite interstate Big Money Set. You see them in New York, Chicago, Houston, Dallas or San Francisco at the ballet, the opera, the museums; they're easy to spot, as they travel in packs and look alike. The whippet-thin women wear Givenchy or Valentino and have their hair done by Mr. Whoever and their eye tucks and face-lifts by Dr. Whoever. The men look sleekly stuffed into their custom-tailored $3,000 Louis suits, which their wives have instructed the tailor to cut skillfully in order to minimize the love handles.

Gayfryd met Saul in November 1982 at the dinner table of Richard Feigen. Now Mr. Feigen is not just the owner of a gallery; he is THE art dealer who mingles with the beautiful people and dwells in elegance in a landmarked townhouse on New York's very posh East Sixty-eighth Street. His companion of the moment is Anne Bass, who is running in heavy competition against upstart Georgette Mosbacher as the doyenne of Houston society. She achieved financial-page fame when billionaire husband Sid Bass paid her a major fortune for the marital divestiture that enabled him to marry his new bride, Mercedes, thereby spawning a series of jokes about how many millions Sid Bass had to pay for an old Mercedes. Anne Bass's patronage of the arts extends beyond Feigen; she just donated one million dollars to the Lincoln Center building campaign. If Richard Feigen is a friend of Gayfryd, then she's running with the right crowd—and that's the first step needed to snare a billionaire.

Picture that first meeting of Saul and Gayfryd. Here we have Saul Steinberg, the forty-three-year-old brilliant billionaire who had already gone through two wives and heaven knows how many bimbos, seated next to a stunning brunette

he had never before met but who was obviously socially acceptable, as she was a friend of the host. He engages her in
polite table banter, which usually begins with the post-wom-
en's-movement opener, "And what do YOU do?" Before
the advent of feminism, you never asked a woman how she
spent her time, lest you wanted to listen to an excruciatingly
boring litany of household chores, good works or children's
achievements. These days, women are achieving on a par
with men and a question about their daily pursuits is quite in
order. Nevertheless, given the cultured household in which
the dinner is being held, Gayfryd's answer to Saul's query
has an eye-opener: "What do I do? I own a steel-pipe business in New Orleans." The picture of this ravishingly feminine creature plodding through steel mills in a hardhat had
to be intriguing. Of course, she was married at the time, but
that never impedes social relationships today, nor did it ever
in those circles where adultery was the indoor sport and polo
the outdoor one.

How gorgeous Gayfryd came to run a steel-pipe business
is the next subject. She was born in 1950 in Vancouver, British Columbia, to middle-class parents. Her father was a tele-
phone-company clerk and her mother a proper stay-at-home
wife who saw to it that her daughter had all the nice advantages such as ballet lessons and a college education. Gayfryd
studied psychology at the University of British Columbia.
While a student, she met and married a young metallurgy
engineer and they moved to South Africa, where she finished
her degree. Coming from the free society of Canada, she was
appalled by apartheid and kept after her husband to find a
job back home in North America. An opportunity arose in
New Orleans, and they moved to Louisiana, where she
found a job in an outpatient clinic for adolescents. As she
tells it, he missed the big open spaces and easier living of
South Africa and she didn't, so they split.

Then she met her first millionaire, Norman Johnson, who
was, as they say, in oil. He was smitten, he was rich, he was

persistent, so they married. After having grown up in the home of a wage earner whose weekly paycheck was carefully budgeted in order to meet the monthly rent, it had to be heady stuff to suddenly find yourself living in the biggest house in New Orleans. The building was so grand that people kept coming to the door under the assumption they had found the local public library. In 1978, she gave birth to a son, Rayne, and continued to live the life of a rich man's wife. But Gayfryd has a brain and with her heightened consciousness felt a restless need to do more. Listening to Norman talk about his business, she picked up on his oft-made statement that women made great salespeople. The oil field operators needed and bought steel pipes, why shouldn't she be the one who would sell them? All she had to do was find a source for stock and then get out there and convince the oil companies to buy from a good-looking woman instead of some beer-bellied good ole boy. She convinced Norman to give her start-up money, and then asked her best friend, Arlene Montgomery Mmahat, the wife of a wealthy attorney, to be her partner. They named the company New Era, which it was for the oil companies, who weren't used to dealing with women. At first they had to locate steel mills that would sell to such unlikely customers, and then find customers who would buy. The going was tough at first as the good-ole-boy network that bought and sold to the oil industry believed a woman's place was at a cotillion and not in commerce. But Gayfryd is a determined and capable woman and would not be deterred. She and her partner persisted until the industry got used to the novelty of dealing with women. The business grew slowly and in 1986 she sold her share for $500,000.

Meanwhile, back at the ranch, husband Norman was destroying his business. He was also indulging in that dangerous, perennially popular all-American game called "Screw the IRS" and was secreting sums offshore that he neglected to report. But someone else did, because suddenly, hot and muggy New Orleans got even hotter for Norman. One day he just didn't show up for dinner. Three weeks later, his frantic wife got a phone call from England. Norman had kicked over the traces, had had a face-lift and was ready for a new life. Gayfryd flew to England to inform him that she didn't like the new Norman, wasn't too big on the old Norman, and wanted a divorce. On the way back home from London through New York, she called her friend Richard Feigen to commiserate. Her timing was perfect; he was going that night to a dinner party at good old Saul Steinberg's, and would she like to come along. Would she ever.

Apparently the host remembered the lovely Canadian with the unusual occupation and seated her at his right. She told him about her pending divorce and he advised her on lawyers. Gayfryd was soon to be a woman-without-a-rich-mate; it was certainly time for renewed action. As she told an interviewer, "You know, I thought, this is a very attractive guy. Anyway, I was looking for someone to be bad with that night and this seemed to be it."

Let's rewind here and examine that statement. Saul Steinberg is not of prepossessing physical stature. He is chubby and short, to boot. But he has a shining smile, a great joie de vivre and the kind of bouncy élan and confidence you exude when you have made your first million at the age of twenty-nine and at forty-three own almost as many properties and companies as the Japanese.

So if Gayfryd found him a very attractive guy, I can buy that. Power is a great aphrodisiac and $400 million certainly gets the juices flowing. If you're feeling blue because you just learned your husband and the father of your child is a felon and, worse, broke, and if at age thirty-two you've racked up two failed marriages and not a hell of a lot of cash, I can understand why your morale could use the pick-me-up of a little libidinous adventure. It certainly must be titillating to be able to make out surrounded by Rodins, Renoirs and Titians and not be thrown out by a museum guard. (Mr. Steinberg's incredible collection of priceless art outnumbers and outclasses the collections of most minor museums in the world.)

Saul Steinberg is a nice, smart Jewish boy from Brooklyn. He graduated from the famous Wharton School of the University of Pennsylvania, now better known as the infamous training ground for junk bond traders and corporate raiders, boasting alumni such as Ronald O. Perelman and Michael Milken. Always precocious, he got his degree at nineteen, and three years later latched onto the unique and timely concept of leasing computers by forming a company called Leasco.

In the 1960s the United States was fat and happy and enjoyed a secure position in the world's competitive structure. We are the first and the best, the attitude was, so let's do a little domestic housecleaning and go after those big bad United States monopolies. The government embarked upon a massive antitrust campaign intended, it said, to protect the consumer. One of the major so-called victories was the break-up of AT&T, which cost the government millions of dollars and left the average American with a legacy of aggravation, inefficiency and expense. Another victory was forcing IBM to sign an antitrust settlement that in part opened up the lucrative business of leasing computers to third parties. Boy wonder Steinberg spotted the opportunity and formed Leasco. He was so far ahead of his time that he was in business alone for almost four years. There was no competition, and he was able to write leases that were virtually riskless: he knew he could get back all of the cost of the equipment, as well as interest. He had no capital; he had to borrow 103 percent of the cost of the equipment. The banks thought he was kidding when he told them he needed 3 percent for operating expenses and 100 percent for IBM.

In 1965 Leasco went public and at age twenty-nine Saul Steinberg was a millionaire. By 1967 he could see that leasing was becoming unprofitable. Too many others had joined the competition, and it was time for him to look for new worlds to conquer. In 1967 he bought the Reliance Insurance Company, which he has used ever since as a base for aggressive investments in a wide variety of companies. His hostile attempt to acquire Chemical Bank in 1969 earned him the title, created for him, of corporate raider. Since then, he has moved into Walt Disney Productions, Flying Tiger Airlines and a host of other corporations.

Steinberg's financial empire today is far-flung and runs into the billions. His brilliance consists of ferreting out hidden assets in companies and then pouncing. He owns or has tried to own everything; his conversation sounds like Monopoly, but with him it's real. For the past few years, he has applied the same level of passion spent in acquiring companies to the buying of art and has become a highly respected collector, patron and philanthropist who has given millions of dollars to the Metropolitan Museum of Art.

When Steinberg met Gayfryd, he was a man who was peaking at age forty-three; he already had all the money he could want, had achieved the fame of being the enfant terrible of Wall Street and fearless leader of the feared and respected corporate takeover corps, he was now out-philanthropizing the Rockefellers, he had children, he had his pick of models and starlets. What he needed now was not just a playmate, but a companion, someone who could share his interests and would understand his business of takeovers and acquisitions, someone he could talk to, someone with whom he could have lots of fun, lots of love and a real, but better-than-Brooklyn home life.

Gayfryd's timing could not have been more perfect. She was stunning, but mature and intelligent—not some sexy airhead. True, she was a shiksa, but not some society, upper-class WASP who wouldn't have a clue about Saul's humble beginnings. Gayfryd might have been a millionaire's wife, but the strong middle-class mores and ethics of her upbringing were compatible to those of Saul's. It was a good fit, and it took.

Gayfryd embarked upon her own acquisition campaign and showed Saul how she could effect a friendly takeover. Wisely, she laid down certain rules for their relationship that immediately set it apart from previous lascivious liaisons and created a pseudo-moral tone. Sure, they slept together—but only on Saturdays and Sundays. That may sound phony puritanical, but it was really practical. As she lived in New Orleans and had a child and home there, she could only get to New York on weekends. She even managed to make a statement about her trips to and from the airport by insisting that he himself take her. ("I don't like being sent off to La Guardia with the chauffeur after a weekend of passion," she said.) By establishing these superficial and somewhat silly guidelines, she was, in effect, endowing herself with a certain dignity that precluded the age-old feminine fear of "But will he respect me in the morning?" To lift the moral tone of their affair further, she insisted on strict fidelity. He wanted her to move in with him, but she refused.

In the meantime, she was still a married woman. In 1983 Norman Johnson was indicted, pleaded guilty to the charge of evading $7 million of income tax and was sentenced to fourteen months in prison. Gayfryd divorced him and in December 1983 married Saul Steinberg. Johnson committed suicide by jumping off a building in Houston in 1985, shortly after his release.

Now Gayfryd moved in and took over Saul's life to his utter and obvious delight. She is a competent, take-charge woman and he obviously loves it and her. In order to cut down on his corpulence, she locks up the kitchen at night so that he can't raid the fridge for a midnight mayonnaise-sandwich nosh. He is no longer a compulsive candy-eater, at least while she's around. Gayfryd has gotten his weight down by schlepping him to spas, such as the Canyon Ranch in Tucson, and with regular dieting and walking programs. He jogs, he walks, he diets—but face it, Gayfryd, not all of us are born with those skinny shiksa genes. Next to his tall slender spouse, Saul still looks like a cute Jewish Pillsbury Dough-boy.

Gayfryd imposes other domestic disciplines. She is a great believer in the sanctity of home, hearth and family; she insists that Saul be home by six so that they can have dinner *en famille*. It is a luxury he probably could not have afforded years ago when he was fighting to make his first million. But one of the perks of being the billionaire boss is you get to take off whenever the hell you want to.

The permanent resident family now consists of one of those modern his-hers-and-ours ménages of thirteen-year-old Rayne Johnson, her son; twelve-year-old Julian, his son; and Holden, their seven-year-old daughter. The five of them sit down to dinner in the ballroom-sized dining room that is just a small part of a three-story apartment boasting an entry hall that is probably twice the size of the lobby of any Brooklyn building.

The apartment has been depicted and drooled over by *Town and Country* and other publications ad nauseam. Once owned by John D. Rockefeller, it has been called baronial, palatial and a Walt Disney Blenheim. How else can you describe a triplex on Park Avenue that has thirty-four huge rooms with walls covered by one of the finest private art collections in the world?

When you enter the apartment, you are greeted with an array of Francis Bacons. In 1985 the Tate Museum in London borrowed the Steinbergs' *Triptych* as the centerpiece of a retrospective exhibition of the great English artist. In the drawing room are Rubens's *The Triumph of Constantine, The Plague of Athens* by the seventeenth-century Flemish painter Michael Sweerts, Rubens's *Venus and the Three Muses Mourning the Death of Adonis*, Titian's *Salome with the Head of John the Baptist* (not one of Gayfryd's favorites) and in the master bedroom are Ernst Kirchner's *Nude* and Paul Klee's *Solar Eclipse*. Throughout the apartment there are Hepworth and Rodin sculptures. Frans Hals is represented. There is a Renoir in the powder room. Saul Steinberg has sixty Barlachs, more than the Barlach Museum in Hamburg. In the gray-flannel-walled poolroom (where Saul enjoys playing pool with his brother Robert, who is president of Reliance Group Holdings, Inc.) is Otto Mueller's *The Seated Couple*. Frequent guests are Philippe de Montebello of the Metropolitan Museum of Art and William Rubin of the Museum of Modern Art.

Unlike many of the new millionaires who amass art by the pound for investment, as an IRS ploy, or to flaunt their self-importance, Steinberg really loves and understands his collection. He speaks with the fanaticism of the true collector. "Unless it strikes me as a painting I have to own, I don't buy it. I'm interested in quality and condition. I will pay for quality. I don't care what the last painting by the same artist cost me. A great painting is a great painting. It's instinct. I go after it."[1]

Gayfryd recognized the importance of her husband's passion for art and has tried to understand and share it. Attacking the situation in the efficient way she handles everything, she commissioned someone at the Met to write in-depth backgrounds of each of their paintings so that she could understand and appreciate them.

When you become the wife of a man with billions, you have to stake out a cause with which you can be identified. It's much more effective and ego-gratifying than just shoving your money into disparate charities. It's like being the wife of a President. Every first lady has chosen a human betterment role. With Barbara Bush, it's illiteracy. Nancy Reagan had her "Just Say No" shtick. With Lady Bird Johnson, it was beautification of the countryside and roads. Jackie Kennedy worked on restoring the historical furnishings of the White House. But much like some actors and comedians who seek an important charity to which they can see their names attached only to find all the diseases taken, Gayfryd had her work cut out for her finding the unique special cause that would be hers alone. Decisions, decisions. Finally, she decided that rather than go for some vague humanitarian organization that required mere money but no mind, or some form of the performing arts that guaranteed center seating and elaborate galas but little participation, she would opt for a cause that involved the brain. As she told *U.S. News & World Report* in 1988, "I decided intellectual anorexia on Park Avenue was not going to be my chief occupation." She announced that the Steinbergs would become the big patrons of PEN, the international organization that fights for writers' rights throughout the world and was one of the most vociferous groups supporting Salman Rushdie.

It all started when she met Norman Mailer and they charmed each other. She thought he was wonderful, and he was surprised by her intelligence. PEN needs money to continue its work and all contributions are gladly accepted. Gayfryd offered to run a little cocktail party to raise funds and invited some Steinberg friends. Saul went around the room calling in favors and within twenty minutes raised $200,000. Mailer was enchanted. The Steinbergs announced their patronage of PEN, and Mailer sat back in delight with the comfort of knowing that his organization's money problems were at an end. He could also pride himself on having found that rarity, a self-effacing supporter who will not demand bronze plaques and trumpeted personalized identification. In fact, Gayfryd made a point of eschewing that role by announcing that she specifically did not want PEN dubbed "Mrs. Steinberg's pet hobby" and is stepping back publicly from PEN because "they need the confidence of knowing other people can attract a crowd."

Everything was idyllic. Norman did his job, Gayfryd did hers and everyone was happy—except for a few member authors with small brains and big mouths who publicly announced their indignation at having their illustrious organization perceived as the protectorate of some rich upstarts who wish to achieve derivative intellectual status by becoming affiliated with the great works and talents of America's leading authors. Apparently these idiots are unaware that the greatest artists in history were supported by patrons. If you need funding, there are two sources—the government and private contributions—if you're looking for the one with the least strings attached, go for private. The media loved the brouhaha caused by the whole affair, and the Steinbergs hated it because it created exactly the image they were trying to avoid, so they announced their withdrawal from PEN sponsorship. Now PEN is reduced to running around scrounging and pleading for financial support and the Steinbergs are seeking other recipients for their largesse.

Gayfryd sits on the board of her husband's alma mater, the Wharton School of the University of Pennsylvania. The Steinbergs have adopted a fifth-grade Harlem class and she visits the children weekly and will eventually pay their college tuition.

Gayfryd does not cut the conventional figure of a rich man's wife in New York's La Cirque crowd; it is a position she seems to try assiduously to avoid. She dresses in clothes by Scaasi and other top designers, but doesn't make it a mandatory part of her agenda to show up at all the fashion shows sitting next to all the same women making careful notes of all the same dresses. Her statements to the press are obviously intended to show her strong desire to be disassociated with the Susan Gutfreund School of Social Status. As she told *U.S. News & World Report*, "You'd think some of the people in this town came from underneath cabbage leaves," alluding to those who obfuscate their roots. "If you go into things feeling you are worthwhile, you don't have to do contrived things." Unlike the cliquish women who make the rounds of the right benefits, she asks to sit next to different people. "They sit next to the same people relentlessly, over and over again, instead of taking a chance. What's the worst that could happen? A little bacteria never hurt anyone."[2]

However, she blew her iconoclastic image with the 1988

wedding of Saul's twenty-six-year-old daughter Laura to thirty-four-year-old Jonathan Tisch, son of Robert Tisch and a nephew of Saul's good friend and fellow zillionaire Lawrence Tisch. Agreed, it was indeed a time for celebration as the families meshed to a level of symbiotic perfection that would have done any nineteenth-century matchmaker proud: the parents were friends, they shared the same religion, and neither of the happy couple could be accused of marrying the other for money. It was described in *Vanity Fair* as "a baronial alliance on the scale of Castile and Aragon in the fifteenth century."

Okay, so you don't hire a hall in Queens and serve mini knishes, but $1 million for flowers? All right, the affair celebrates a significant merger between two Wall Street ruling families, but does it have to cost as much as a coronation? Then in August of the same year, Saul hit the big fifty and Gayfryd threw an extravaganza that was estimated to cost $10,000 per person. And the guest list numbered 250. The party was held in the Steinberg's Long Island weekend house, which has been described as a white clapboard ocean liner. Indicative of the Steinbergs' maverick-socialite stance is the unchic Hampton location of their place: it's not in East Hampton or Southampton, but on Quogue. Of course, that did not tarnish the stellar quality of the guest list, which included Barbara Walters, Senator Alfonse D'Amato and Vartan Gregorian.

The event was deemed so excessive that it rated two articles in the *Washington Post* and an editorial in the *New York Times*. Perhaps the press was bothered by the spectacle of the replica of a seventeenth-century Flemish house adorned with ten animated tableaux composed of live models, including a nude representation of Rembrandt's *Danae*. Or the twin mermaids swimming in the acre-sized swimming pool. Or the five-tiered birthday cake flanked by two live cherubs. Or the beautiful Oriental rugs tossed over the grass to ease the guests' mobility. The entire affair smacked of the kind of entertainments Marie Antoinette threw regularly for her little Louis and that you can now pay to see replicated at the son et lumière performances at Versailles. The press referred to "wretched excess," but the guests were delighted. One wonders what sort of gift one brings to the birthday boy at such a fete. When you know your hostess has spent ten thousand bucks for your presence, you can't show up carrying a box of cheese danish.

The capping comment as reported by the media was Saul's gratefully touching tribute to his wife, whom he toasted with "Honey, if this moment were stock, I'd short it." To which the little woman answered, "My mother always says, 'Don't tell people you love them, show them.' And this is my way of saying, 'I love you.' "

The madness here is that within their financial frame of reference, it all makes perfect sense. My cleaning woman, whose husband works as a day laborer, spent $50,000 on her daughter's wedding. If you consider the proportion of their total worth that these hard-working people spent on what they consider an important occasion, Gayfryd's blowing a mere 2.5 million dollars on Saul's milestone birthday is perfectly acceptable. What the hell, if you can't have fun spending your money, what good is having it?

I have seen Gayfryd Steinberg thrown into the hopper of Trophy Wives: I don't believe she fits into that category. For one thing, she is only eleven years younger than her husband; there is not the usual two-decade disparity that separates the other women generationally from their spouses. Also, the Steinbergs are plainly wild about each other; his millions certainly affected his attractiveness, but affection was also a major factor, as she is, in the opinion of all who know them, very much in love. Also unlike the usual nouvelle wife brigade, she is very concerned with family and considers raising well-adjusted children a major responsibility. As she said, "One of the most unattractive things about the wealthy is that they think they deserve to be."[3] She is constantly aware of the well-publicized mayhem among the superrich such as drug busts, money fights and suicides and is trying hard to prevent such occurrences in her brood. She is worried that the presence of tremendous wealth can sap their drive for achievement—something that usually happens with the nouveau riche but has been bred out of old money families such as the Rockefellers, who have instilled a sense of responsibility in all members of the family.

Most Trophy Wives regard children as a hindrance that interferes with their full-time jobs of creating fun, fun, fun lives for their senior-citizen husbands who have already been through the domestic anguish of raising kids. If there are preexistent offspring, they give them as wide a berth as possible and if they decide to procreate, the new offspring is relegated to a competent nanny. Gayfryd Steinberg is not of that mold. Like all new wives of tycoons, she is out to make a good life for her husband, but unlike the others, she does not try to create some phony fairy-tale existence that is totally divorced from their previous reality. You get the sense that she is trying to get Saul to lose weight not so that he should look more like Cary Grant, but because it's healthier. She treats her life as though she is there to stay, unlike the others, who, like Scheherazade, feel they will be discarded once they lose their entertainment value.

What has Gayfryd got that caught Saul Steinberg? Obviously everything he needed, whether he knew it or not.

References

1. "Barony on Park Avenue," Wendy Moonan, *Town & Country*, November 1985, p. 238.
2. "The Talk of the Town" column, *U. S. News & World Report*, February 1988, p. 81.

CHAPTER IX

ALMA MAHLER

The Viennese
Genius-Collector

WHEN IT COMES TO RANKING ENTRANTS in any competition for who has amassed the most famous husbands, Alma Mahler sets the standard by which all others are measured. Her stunning matrimonial record has been immortalized in song by the Harvard professor/folksinger Tom Lehrer.

> *The loveliest girl in Vienna*
> *Was Alma, the smartest as well.*
> *Once you picked her up on your antenna*
> *You'd never be free of her spell.*
>
> *Her lovers were many and varied*
> *From the day she began the beguine.*
> *There were three famous ones whom she married*
> *And God knows how many between.*
>
> *Alma, tell us,*
> *All modern women are jealous,*
> *Which of your magical wands*
> *Got you Gustav and Walter and Franz?*

Alma Mahler. *(Courtesy of the Alma Mahler-Werfel Collection, Special Collections Dept., Van Pelt Library)*

The first one she married was Mahler,
Whose buddies all knew him as Gustav.
And each time he saw her he'd holler,
"Ach, that is the fräulein I must haff!"

Their marriage however was murder.
He'd scream to the heavens above,
"I'm writing Das Lied von der Erde,
And she only wants to make love."

Alma, tell us,
All modern women are jealous,
You should have a statue in bronze
For bagging Gustav and Walter and Franz.

While married to Gus she met Gropius,
And soon she was swinging with Walter.
Gus died and her teardrops were copious,
She cried all the way to the altar.

But he would work late at the Bauhaus,
And only came home now and then.
She said, "Vat am I running, a chowhouse?
It's time to change partners again."

Alma, tell us,
All modern women are jealous.
Though you didn't even use Ponds,
You got Gustav and Walter and Franz.

While married to Walt she'd met Werfel,
And he too was caught in her net.
He married her, but he was careful,
'Cause Anna was no Bernadette.

And that is the story of Alma,
Who knew how to receive and to give.
The body that reached her embalma
Was one that had known how to live.

Alma Mahler around the time of her marriage to Gustav Mahler. *(Courtesy of the Alma Mahler-Werfel Collection, Special Collections Dept., Van Pelt Library)*

Alma, tell us,
How can they help being jealous?
Ducks always envy the swans
Who get Gustav and Walter—you never did falter—
With Gustav and Walter and Franz.

Alma Maria Schindler Mahler Gropius Werfel is the legendary multiple-marrier of all time and the hands-down winner of any contest of who can attract and acquire the most geniuses within a single lifetime. Her X-rated exploits have been chronicled in books, magazines and newspapers, as well as in song. According to an article that appeared on February 14, 1982, in the Valentine's Day edition of the *Washington Post*, "Alma Schindler Mahler Gropius Werfel was, you might say, the Liz Taylor of the Bauhaus." The main difference between Liz and Alma, however, is that one look at Elizabeth Taylor's stunning, voluptuous beauty and no one questions, "What has SHE got?" whereas Alma may have been the darling of the Danube, but she was no more than a pretty fräulein who looked like she had enjoyed lots of *schlag mit* her strudel. Yet, with no obviously discernible attractions, she not only married three men, each of whom was a genius in a different field, but also had love affairs with practically all the creative men in Central Europe.

This is Alma's marital menu in chronological order: (1) Gustav Mahler, the immortal composer and conductor (1902-1911); (2) Walter Gropius, the internationally famous architect who founded the Bauhaus School that revolutionized interior design (1915-1920); (3) Franz Werfel, the celebrated poet, playwright and author of *The Song of Bernadette* (later made into a movie), the hit Broadway play *Jacobowsky and the Colonel* and many, many more (1929-1945).

Throughout these with-benefit-of-clergy alliances, Alma managed to maintain an affair with the famous artist Oskar Kokoschka, who remained her friend and lover until her death at age eighty-five, not to mention little sexual sideline sorties with Gerhart Hauptmann, the dramatist; Paul Kammerer, the biologist; and Ossip Gabrilowitsch, the pianist, conductor and, later, husband of Clara Clemens, daughter of Mark Twain.

What did she have that, even when getting on in years (she was fifty when she married thirty-nine-year-old Franz Werfel), outshone the competition of younger, more beautiful women who vied for the love and attention of these giants in their fields?

Was she gorgeous? No. She was five feet three inches and weighed in at 140 pounds, which would be considered slightly zaftig by today's standards. She has been described as having a sturdy figure (a euphemism for a shapeless chubbo) with a waist that needed corsets to make it look fashionably small. She had an imposing chin, a shapely but not small nose and lovely blue eyes. As years went on and the legend of Alma Mahler grew, she was repeatedly referred to as "the most beautiful girl in Vienna," a title to which she was hardly entitled but which was probably coined by some journalist who figured she had to be a knockout if she was the chosen betrothed of Gustav Mahler, the musical toast of Europe. Many undeserved labels have been created by over-eager newsmen who seek to put romance and color into stories by endowing their subjects with mythical beauty and charm. After all, who wants to read about an ugly heroine? Alma was pretty, but certainly not the possessor of head-turning looks or, in fact, any special qualities that would seem to attract men.

But there certainly had to be some secret to which this woman was privy that made her desirable to outstanding men throughout her life.

Alma Maria Schindler was born in 1879 to a mother who had occasionally sung soprano in minor operettas and a father who became one of the most popular landscape painters of his era by turning out an oeuvre that pleased the wealthy nobility. Alma adored her father and perceived Jakob Emil

Schindler as a genius, an attitude not shared by the world.
The popularity of his work did not outlast his lifetime, but it
did earn him a posthumously erected statue in the city park.
Alma's continued obsession with him was evidenced by the
postcards of his statue that she sent to friends throughout her
entire life.

As with other women described in this book, a much-idol-
ized father became the influential force in the daughter's attitude toward men. Whether her father was in fact the supe-
rior being she thought he was is unimportant. In her
emotionally skewed mind, he was a giant among men and
the model she sought to replicate in her husbands and lovers.
Sigmund Freud, a friend of Gustav Mahler, told him, "I
know your wife. She loved her father and she can only
choose and love a man of his sort."[1]

Alma Schindler came of age in Vienna, the city that was
the cultural center of Europe. Mozart, Beethoven, Schubert,
Brahms, Bruckner and Strauss were all tied in with its artistic
traditions, and theatres and concert halls were important
parts of Viennese life. New York City has two major opera
houses, yet few of its citizens are aware of their programs.
But in turn-of-the-century Vienna, almost everyone, rich or
poor, could tell you what opera was being presented on any
given night. The coffeehouses were the heart of the city and
there you heard cultural and political gossip, intellectual conversation and philosophical speculation. In this milieu, it was
natural for all young men and women to study the arts. Alma
had lessons in painting and drawing and then began to study
musical composition with Alexander von Zemlinsky, a musician whose works are only now being rediscovered. When
Alma went to his house for lessons, she frequently met a
shabby young fellow student named Arnold Schönberg and
there began a friendship with this now world-famous composer that lasted for over fifty years. Alma composed more
than a hundred songs and several instrumental pieces and
developed a lifelong dedication to music. Who, then, should

be of greater interest to her than the famed Gustav Mahler, the acclaimed composer and director of the Vienna Court Opera and the most revered musical figure in the city?

Gustav Mahler was the eldest son of Bernard Mahler, a poor man who had worked his way up from peddler to owner of a distillery. In the age-old Jewish tradition of fostering respect for learning and culture, Bernard did everything in his power to develop his son's outstanding talent as a pianist. Gustav, however, was drawn to conducting and composing and enrolled simultaneously at the University and the Conservatory of Vienna. At age twenty, he began to conduct throughout the country and then moved on to the opera in Prague. He became musical director of the Royal Opera in Budapest, and in 1891 began a six-year engagement in Hamburg. The logical next step was the Vienna Court Opera. He was considered for the prestigious directorship. No one was too concerned about his extreme youth or the unfamiliarly modern quality of his compositions. The only deterrent was the fact that Herr Mahler was a Jew. Years later, Adolph Hitler did not have to create the virulent anti-Semitism that led to the Holocaust; he merely had to reach into the hearts of the Austrians and Germans and reap the harvest of hatred that lay therein. Cosima Wagner, the widow of the composer, would not allow the directorship of the Vienna Opera to be given to a Jew, even though the brilliant Mahler was already recognized as a great conductor of Wagner's works. So prevalent was this oppression of Jews that nobody saw any irony or injustice in her edict, including Mahler, who, following the groveling response forced on so many of his victimized people throughout history, bowed to her dictum by converting to Christianity in 1897.

Alma met Gustav Mahler at a dinner party and claimed she was drawn to him immediately. Why not? Not only was he a vibrant, attractive man, but he was one of the reigning geniuses of Europe's vibrant music world. Their first meeting has been described in many books, all derived from Alma's own version, which leans heavily on her clever conversation and compelling charm. Alma Mahler was never known for her lack of self-confidence. In her book *Life and Letters of Gustav Mahler*, she wrote: "From the first moment, Mahler observed me closely, not simply because of my face, which might have been called beautiful in those days, but also because of my piquant air."[2]

She indicated that she and Mahler engaged in cultivated banter that ranged from the philosophical to the interpretive and, of course, as this is her reconstruction of events, she recounts a number of statements that seem highly intelligent and remarkably poised for a young woman of twenty-one to have made to a forty-year-old national idol.

Mahler's interest in her was not surprising. She was fresh-faced, pretty, a young twenty-one to his forty, and gentile, always a magnetic quality to a Jew who wishes to escape his Jewishness. Alma was also on his cultural level and of his world. In her books, she made a great deal of her musical compositions and considered herself a fine composer manqué, although none of her works indicate anything other than a mediocre ability. This was undoubtedly a large part of her attraction for Mahler. Powerful men like their women to have talent, as long as it is minor and unthreatening, because such spouses are more understanding of the great men's needs, more appreciative of their genius and better able to help them in their work. The author goes for a reverent young writer who can type and edit his manuscripts, the painter is drawn to an awed young artist who can help him evaluate his work and take care of dealing with the galleries, the actor is attracted to an adoring aspirant who helps him select and learn scripts, the maestro/composer seeks a wife who copies his compositions and liberates him from the drudgery of life's minutia. The first statement Mahler made to Alma about possible marriage was: "It's not so simple to marry a person like me. I am free and must be free. I cannot be bound, or tied to one spot. My job at the opera is simply from one day to the next."

She answered, "Of course. Don't forget that I am the child of artists and have always lived among artists and, also, I'm one myself. What you say seems to me obvious."[3]

The degree of dedication he required from her became apparent even before they were married when she cut short a letter she was writing to him with the explanation that she was involved in finishing a musical composition and therefore could not take the time to write him a long letter. He wrote back in indignant fury, fuming that she would even consider giving anything priority over the far more important fulfillment of his needs, and he forbade her to compose any more.

If a man in the 1990s tried that on a woman, she would be out the door in a shot. But Alma merely sobbed to her mother and then acquiesced. As she put it: "I buried my dreams and perhaps it was for the best. It has been my privilege to give my creative gifts another life in minds greater than my own."[4]

Later along in life, she had some doubts. In *My Life, My Loves*, she remonstrated with Mahler over his lack of concern and respect for her feelings: "I told Gustav how hurt I am by his utter disinterest in what goes on inside me. My knowledge of music, for instance, suits him only as long as I use it for him. He answered: 'Is it my fault that your budding dreams have not come true?' "[5]

Alma also had a special asset that served her well with men all her life. She was slightly hard of hearing due to a childhood bout with measles. As a result, she always leaned in closely to the person who was speaking, thus conveying a posture of intimate concern and a flattering eagerness to listen that men found utterly beguiling.

Gustav was obviously smitten with young Alma the evening of the dinner party, and their relationship moved ahead rapidly. In light of today's matrimonial mores, it is always rather startling to realize that marriage was discussed so openly and so early in a relationship years ago, but of course, in those days, it was the only socially acceptable consummation. Three weeks after their meeting he proposed marriage and she accepted.

To Mahler, she was a lovely young Christian girl who would adore and take care of him, thus replacing his sister Justine, who had been his loving but somewhat resentful housekeeper, as she had a long-standing affair with the concertmaster of the Vienna Philharmonic but had denied herself the pleasures of marriage and family because of what she felt to be her obligation to Gustav. He was seeking a malleable young woman whom he could mold into the companion he required, and Alma was the ideal clay. Mahler made his requirements perfectly clear in this letter to her: "Although you're an adorable, infinitely enchanting young girl with an upright soul and a richly talented, frank and already self-assured person, you are still not a personality. That which you are to me, Alma, that which you could perhaps be, or become—the dearest and most sublime object of my life, the loyal and courageous companion who understands and promotes me, my stronghold invulnerable to enemies from both within and without, my peace, my heaven in which I can constantly immerse myself, find myself again and rebuild myself."[6]

He let her know that her small musical talent was never again to be taken seriously, as it would intrude upon the services and devotion he expected, and that their life would have to be totally involved with his work.

"Would it be possible for you, from now on, to regard MY music as YOURS? . . . One thing is certain and that is that you must become 'what I need' if we are to be happy together, i.e., my wife, not my colleague. . . . The role of 'composer' falls to me . . . yours is that of the loving companion and understanding partner. . . . You must give yourself to me UNCONDITIONALLY, shape your future life, in every detail, entirely in accordance with my needs and desire nothing in return save my LOVE."[7]

Alma Mahler always depicted herself as an independent woman and seemed to see no conflict with that self-image and the total acceptance of Mahler's clearly stated terms for their marriage, which truly stretches the concept of self-delusion to its limit. The fact that she went ahead with the marriage after receiving those dicta is an indication of Alma's compelling greed to be the wife of a great man.

They were married on March 9, 1902, and immediately Alma learned what her life would be as Madame Mahler. She enjoyed all the flowers, gifts, notes and newspaper notoriety. But there was a great deal of adjustment required to adapt to Gustav's relentless regimen. He rose at seven, had breakfast, worked on his music, went to the opera at nine, lunched at one, relaxed and went for a long walk, took tea at five and returned to the opera, where he stayed well into the evening. Then he came home for a late supper, spent some time reading, talking or playing duets with Alma, then went to sleep. Alma's role as wife to the maestro involved insulating him from all the niggling details of life, which meant waiting for the daily call from his assistant to inform her that Mahler was on the way home for lunch, so that steaming soup would be on the table when he walked through the door. She was expected to be at the opera to meet him at the end of the day and in the director's box whenever he was conducting. She devoted herself to him but the rewards were worth it to her; she enjoyed a life of fame and financial ease as his international reputation grew. Her daughter Maria was born in 1902 and Gustav was a delighted, doting parent. A second daughter, Anna, was born two years later.

As Gustav had promised, Alma had the secondary satisfaction of participating in his music by facilitating his output. While Gustav composed his Fifth Symphony, she copied, occasionally filling in notes that had been merely sketched. When he completed a movement, he played it on the piano and discussed it with her. As he had predicted in his pre-nuptial letter, his music became their life and it was an excit-ing and rewarding existence. In 1907 Mahler was invited to conduct at the Metropolitan Opera and they moved to New York City and became part of the thrilling music scene of the era. They lived at the Savoy Hotel, where many famous Met-ropolitan Opera singers lived, including Enrico Caruso, who was a frequent guest in their home. Constant traveling was a requirement of Mahler's position, and they made many At-lantic crossings and trips throughout the United States and Europe. Finally, Alma found herself on the verge of exhaus-tion, and her doctor suggested she have a stay at a spa in Toblebad, Germany.

Spa stays were quite common in those days for women who complained of an assortment of vague ailments usually attributed to various organs in the body such as the liver, gall bladder and heart. Undoubtedly many of these illnesses were gynecological in origin, an area never mentioned in polite company, and usually resulted in prescriptions for prolonged retreats to one of the spas or other undefined curative cen-ters that dotted Europe.

Alma enjoyed her months of freedom from the tyrannical demands of Mahler and his career, especially when she met a fellow spa resident named Walter Gropius, who responded ardently to the fabled Alma charm. Gropius was twenty-seven (three years younger than Alma), a handsome archi-tect from a highly respected German family. With her unerr-ing nose for genius, she recognized that he had extraordinary vision and talent and would some day accomplish great things. Coming from a different art discipline, Gropius was somewhat ignorant of the music world and assumed that Alma Mahler was the daughter of the great Gustav. Less than a week after Alma returned home, a letter arrived for Gustav Mahler from Walter Gropius asking for the hand of his daughter, Alma, in marriage! As one would imagine, the ordure hit the fan in the Mahler domicile. Alma took the opportunity to complain to Gustav that he treated her as a functionary rather than a wife and lover, demanding service and giving few signs of affection and attention in return. Even their lovemaking was done for his pleasure and convenience; forget foreplay and postcoital coziness—he preferred to come to her when she was deeply asleep, take his pleasure and take off. They discussed their differences and worked them out. But nobody thought of answering the adoring swain, who one day turned up on their doorstep. Gustav led him into the house and told Alma to make her choice. She chose Gustav and sent Gropius packing, which did not stop him from sending her a stream of worshipful telegrams along his route home.

In 1911, while conducting in New York, Mahler contracted a streptococcus infection. Having a chronically weak heart, his body could not cope with the assault, and his family, believing as do many people that their own nation offered the best medical care, transported him back to Europe for further treatment and consultation. On May 18, 1911, the famous conductor and composer died in Vienna.

At thirty-one, Alma Mahler was the widow of a world-class genius. Now, besides the indefinable Alma allure, we add the impressive cachet of the Mahler name. It was a magic mix and equipped Alma to embark upon a mating career of Olympic stature.

In 1912 she was introduced to a poor, wildly emotional young artist who was being viewed as a genius in the art world of Vienna, where his temperament and stunning work had caused frequent eruptions. Oskar Kokoschka was one of those multitalented men who shine in many areas, but his supreme skill was in drawing and painting. He was invited to paint a portrait of Carl Moll, Alma's stepfather, and she asked to meet him. Alma, as we know, was turned on only by geniuses, and Kokoschka sounded like a likely candidate for her attention. Not only was he a brilliant artist, but he was seven years younger, good-looking, articulate and highly sexual—all elements lacking in her life with Mahler. She fell in love with Kokoschka at first sight (she seemed to do a lot of that, as her diaries indicated, but perhaps that's the kind of romantic twaddle that women of that era were expected to enter in their diary pages) and asked him to paint her portrait, certainly a clever device to assure his company for a protracted period.

This affair turned out to be the most constant love in her life and became a powerful relationship for both of them that survived the turmoil of lovers, wives and husbands. It was an ideally symbiotic affair: she offered financial support and entrée into the highest cultural circles of Europe; he offered great sex and the thrill of genius. Alma was a big one for preserving the facade of respectability; public profligacy was not her style, so Oskar was rarely permitted to stay the night after sex, and when he visited her country house, she insisted upon separate bedrooms.

Oskar wanted to marry Alma, but there was a major obstacle—his mother. Madame Kokoschka regarded Alma as a grand whore who would ruin her beloved son's promising future, and she fought the union like a fierce lioness defending her cub. She frequently proclaimed that she herself had put too much into her talented son to allow his genius to be sapped and destroyed by a woman recognized by all other women as a self-centered bitch.

Zdenka Podhajsky, a Czechoslovakian woman who was a longtime active member of Vienna's music world and a close friend of Oskar and his sister, tells with great amusement of how the city buzzed with the story of the way in which Madame Kokoschka prevented the marriage of Oskar and Alma.

"The date had been set, the guests invited, and they were going to the magistrate, but the mother was a very resolute woman. The morning of the wedding day, she went to her son's room and locked him in. She stood outside his door and kept repeating, 'You will not go!' He pleaded and yelled, but she said, 'No, you won't go,' and stayed there the whole day. He couldn't jump out the window because it was so high, so the ceremony was canceled because nobody came.

"Next day, Oskar's sister told me that her mother went to the house of Alma Mahler and told the bakery boy who delivered morning rolls and pastries, 'Tell Madame Mahler that the mother of Kokoschka is in front of her house with a revolver and if she doesn't let my boy alone I will shoot her.' Alma Mahler left Vienna after that and eventually Kokoschka followed, but they never married."

Madame Podhajsky mentioned many times that Alma Mahler had "sex appeal" and men always responded to her, even in her old age. As she put it, although Madame Mahler was not all that beautiful or stunning, she had something that drew all men to her side. "A friend once said that every young girl should have the chance to take lessons from Alma on soothing the male ego. She knew how to make friends, lovers and husbands feel important, as if they were the only ones in her life, and as if they had forever to court her to prove their commitment to their work."[8]

In her book, Alma refers to Oskar's undying love and devotion. When I mentioned this to Madame Podhajsky, she laughed and said, "Ah yes, of course. That is her version. Oskar married later on and I saw him many times and he never mentioned Alma Mahler. When her book came out, he was terribly angry and wanted to sue her because many of the things she said about him were untrue."

However, an immortal testament to their relationship, *Die Windsbraut*, dated 1914, hangs in the Basel Museum, showing Alma sleeping in filmy garb with her head on Oskar's shoulder. He is gazing anxiously in the distance, obviously not as relaxed as she—perhaps an indication of his concern about their future.

When war broke out in 1914, it gave Oskar the chance to break free of Alma. He went off to battle, and she was ready to find a new man. Remembering the handsome young architect who had once courted her, Alma learned he was in Berlin and traveled there to work her wiles on unsuspecting Walter Gropius. Once she located him, she applied the full force of her skills and charms to rekindle the dormant spark. Alma decided she wanted Walter as her husband and as the father of future sure-to-be-beautiful children, as he was a very good-looking man. On August 18, 1915, Alma married Walter Gropius, the talented, handsome Aryan.

The day after the wedding, she wrote in her diary, "Yesterday I was married. I have landed. Nothing will move me from my chosen course—clear and pure is my will, and I want nothing but to make this noble man happy! I am satisfied, excited and happy as never before. God preserve my love!"[9] Here we see a woman so supremely self-involved that not only does she endow her selfish aims with purity, but fully expects the Almighty to endorse her efforts.

Among Alma Mahler's less lovely traits was her mindless anti-Semitism. Throughout her diaries and books, she refers to Jews in the most primitive and ignorant ways. According to her convoluted theological analyses, her strength came from being born a Christian, which gave her certain inherent attitudes and traits that were naturally denied any Jew. In her view, Mahler's conversion could not erase the fact that he could never bear the sterling superiority that is Christian. She feared that being Madame Mahler stigmatized her and made her part of that amorphous anomaly called the "Jewish Problem." In her simplistic reasoning, she saw her marriage to the gentile Gropius as a way to release her from the onus of Mahler's Jewishness.

Alma's unerring eye for genius was again right on the mark. Although he was a young, unproven architect when she first met him, Gropius developed into a brilliant innovator who created the unique concept of expressing beauty through industrial buildings and designs that showed, rather than concealed, their purpose. To that end, he founded and

directed Germany's famous Bauhaus School, whose designs
are still highly valued and visible today. His first major buildings, the Fagus factory buildings at Alfeld, Germany in 1912,
had steel frames and glass walls and were viewed as among
the most advanced examples of the architecture of the time.
In 1919, four years after his marriage to Alma, he established the Bauhaus at Weimar in order to integrate and coor-
dinate the building arts. He brought leading architects,
craftsmen and artists to teach design and create industrial
products and buildings. Among the great men involved with
the Bauhaus movement were Paul Klee, Josef Albers and
Marcel Breuer. In later years, Gropius came to the United
States, where he was chairman of the department of architecture at Harvard and designed many major works.

The marriage was a strange one for Alma. She was accus-
tomed to the role of wife on duty twenty-four hours a day,
who dedicates herself to serving the needs of her husband.
But this was a very different man and a different time.
Gropius was a soldier fighting a war, which meant she saw
him only at the brief intervals when he came home on leave.
She described the marriage as "the oddest I could imagine.
So unmarried, so free and yet so bound!"[10]

But she did see him often enough to become pregnant and
one year later gave birth to another daughter, Manon
Gropius. She was overjoyed at becoming a mother again, but
less than delighted with her marriage. Walter was the perfect
reserved, upper middle-class German gentleman. Other than
an outburst here and there of Teutonic temper, such as dashing one of the fans on which Kokoschka had painted Alma's
likeness into the fireplace, life with Walter was boring. Alma
enjoyed the explosive give-and-take emotional behavior of
the creative people who had populated Mahler's world. Although a great part of Walter's appeal to Alma had been his
Christianity, in reality she preferred the company of Jews. As
she stated in later life, she could live neither with Jews nor
without them. She created a tradition of holding salons at

home on Sundays and inviting her musician friends. Alma heard about a rising young poet, Franz Werfel, and, always tuned in to all candidates of genius potential within a radius of a hundred miles, she asked her friend Franz Blei to bring the promising prodigy to her next salon.

The twenty-seven-year-old Werfel was on his way to becoming a major literary figure. While in the army, he had been given special attention by the commanding officers who recognized his growing reputation as one of the best young poets writing in the German language, which made life more pleasant for a young man who had been brought up in pampered comfort as the only son of Rudolf Werfel, head of a prosperous international glove-making company. When Werfel arrived at Alma's apartment, she was not excessively impressed with his appearance. She described the events in her diary with the usual pro and anti-Semitic contradictory approach: "Werfel is a rather fat Jew with full lips and watery almond eyes. But he becomes more and more attractive . . . his unorthodox love of humanity and speech such as, 'How can I be happy when there is someone, somewhere who is suffering . . .' "11

By the fifth of January, just three months later, Alma was already embroiled in a passionate love affair with Werfel. She was a little concerned about the eleven-year age discrepancy between them, but apparently he wasn't. To preserve her good name, an important factor for a married woman of significant reputation, she visited him frequently in his hotel room under the guise of helping him with the galleys of his book. Apparently she was more concerned about taking precautions for propriety than against pregnancy; she soon learned she was going to have a baby, which she told Walter was his.

Their infant son was born prematurely and Franz was beside himself with delight at his fatherhood and fear for the life of his sickly son (who did not survive). At first Walter believed the baby was his and that Franz's avid attentiveness to Alma was just that of a concerned friend of the family. But Walter was no dummy, and soon recognized the signs and the fact that he was on his way out of Alma's life.

In Alma's recollections, Walter alternately accepted the cuckoldry in quiet gentlemanly fashion, or fell to his knees to plead for her forgiveness, a posture hard to picture for the proud and regal architect. For what sin did he need forgiveness? Alma's penchant for viewing herself as faultless probably inclined her to think that her husband should blame his own lack of attentiveness as the cause of his wife's adultery. Most of her recorded allusions are to Gropius's honorable, admirable behavior in the matter. My reading of the facts is that Walter really didn't give a damn. He was at that time heavily involved with plans for building the Bauhaus (meaning "house of architecture") in Germany. He might have liked to discuss the exciting new project with his wife, but she had no interest in architecture and design, just as he had none in her music. At this point, neither had any place in the other's life and their marriage had become a mere facade.

On July 6, 1929, fifty-year-old Alma Marie Schindler Mahler Gropius married thirty-nine-year-old Franz Werfel, and they moved into a twenty-eight-room mansion she bought in Vienna with a studio on the top floor for Franz and a music room for herself.

Three years later, Franz visited with H. G. Wells, Sinclair Lewis and Dorothy Thompson, who was the first of many journalists expelled by the Nazis. He had already experienced some of the virulent outbreaks of anti-Semitism, but now heard firsthand of Hitler's atrocities. Soon Franz's books were being burned and Mahler's music was being banned and the Werfels realized that escape was necessary. For an acclaimed artist, this was not too difficult. In the fall of 1935, Franz and Alma sailed for the United States, where Franz had been invited to oversee the production of his play, *The Eternal Road*, a biblical saga with a musical score by Kurt Weill that had been ordered a year earlier by the famed Max Reinhardt. At the same time, Franz's book *Forty Days of Musa Dagh* was published in America and sold what was then considered an astronomical 200,000 copies in the United States alone. He was on the way to international fame and acclaim. Once again, Alma had hit the genius jackpot.

But now, she had to face the one element in life that even she could not control—aging. Her indestructible vanity led her to develop a style that she thought distracted from the fact that she was now a matronly woman in her fifties. She became very blonde and wore only V-neck black dresses with full sleeves to cover the aging arms, flared skirts to hide the thickening body but short enough to display the still shapely legs. Over these she always wore one of a variety of loose silk-brocade jackets. Her feet were always encased in black wedgies enabling her to move across floors with ease when her hearing difficulty and/or alcohol impaired her balance. Under her clothes she always wore embroidered pink slips, and no panties ever—a point she stated often and proudly.

Eventually, the Werfels settled in California. With the tremendous success of his book *The Song of Bernadette*, which was the March 1942 Book-of-the-Month selection and was later made into a highly successful movie, introducing Jennifer Jones, Franz and Alma became accepted members of Hollywood's film community. At a party they met Luise Rainer, the Academy Award-winning Viennese actress who had vied unsuccessfully to play the title role in Franz's film, and her husband Clifford Odets, the playwright. That same party introduced Alma to Erich Maria Remarque, the author of *All Quiet on the Western Front* and many other famous works, who later married the movie star Paulette Goddard. Alma and he developed a lasting relationship based on similar backgrounds and drinking habits; he kept pouring his vodka and she, her Benedictine.

The Werfels' house at 610 North Bedford Drive in Beverly Hills was filled with members of the growing colony of

Eastern European expatriate artists such as Marlene Dietrich, Arnold Schönberg, Max Reinhardt, the composer Erich Korngold, Lotte Lehmann and Thomas Mann. The place looked like a little piece of Vienna, as Alma managed to have a good many of her possessions shipped there. Werfel was at work on a play that would become the Broadway hit *Jacobowsky and the Colonel*, and Alma tried to ease his life, as she had Mahler's, by handling some of the time-consuming business details. However, she was now thirty years older, a good bit deafer and a lot more dependent on Benedictine—not a good combination when you are working out deals with agents and publishers. As a result, she ended up selling one set of rights to *The Song of Bernadette* several times over, thereby effectively putting an end to her short career as business manager.

On August 26, 1945, Franz Werfel died of a heart attack at home. At the funeral service, the famous conductor Bruno Walter, their friend and neighbor, played Schubert. The mourners included Otto Preminger, Otto Klemperer, Igor Stravinsky and Thomas Mann. Alma sold the Beverly Hills house and moved to New York City, where she bought the building at 120 East Seventy-third Street in which she died at age eighty-six in 1964.

The basis of Alma Mahler's allure has never been fully explained and perhaps never will be because, like all legends, it builds upon itself. But there are certainly many factors that may have contributed to the effectiveness of her achievements.

As with all careers, the toughest part is getting the first job. Alma got Gustav, and that was the master stroke on which her future was based. Once she became Madame Mahler, her reputation in Europe was made, and men saw her adorned with the desirable aura of Mrs. Maestro. After all, it's quite a coup to bed the wife of one of the most acclaimed artists in the world.

Then we have that certain something some women are

blessed with at birth that draws men like moths to a flame. It is definable—it's called sexiness. Nowadays we speak freely of women who are adept at giving great blow jobs, but in Alma's era one never mentioned private parts, let alone ways to deal with them, so we really don't know what magic she exerted in the bedroom. The only substantial clue to her strong sexuality comes from the fact that she made a big thing out of never wearing underpants. A recent article in the *New England Journal of Medicine* describes a marriage that broke up because the husband demanded that his wife never wear underwear. Apparently the image of her near-nudity turned him on, but she found running around without panties unpleasant, if not slightly drafty. There is a sexiness in going barebottomed, a constant awareness of your genitalia, that is automatically communicated to men. So when our adorable Alma leaned toward a man in order to hear him more clearly, her own consciousness of her near nakedness titillated her and undoubtedly subconsciously conveyed her readiness to the panting recipient of her attentions.

Then we have the interesting fact that this overtly anti-Semitic woman married two Jews who both suffered from the self-hatred felt by all who either deny their Jewishness and convert, as did Mahler, or accept anti-Semitic abuse, as did Werfel. Marrying a Christian who openly and constantly scorns you as inferior because you do not carry the superlative blood and genes of the pure Aryan handles your shame in two ways: (1) by marriage, you have captured and thus conquered a gentile, thereby implicitly proving your actual superiority; (2) by being subjected to her disdain daily, you are feeding your own self-detestation full-time. It makes one wonder if her marriage to Gropius was a failure because Alma missed these stimulating dynamics.

Stripping away the mystique of legends is of questionable value. Perhaps it's best to preserve our illusions, and maybe that's what Alma's grand allure was—just an illusion. But everybody bought it, so it sure as hell worked for her.

References

1. Alma Mahler, *Life and Letters of Gustav Mahler*, London: John Murray, 1946, p. 147.
2. *Ibid.*, p. 2.
3. *Ibid.*, p. 15.
4. *Ibid.*, p. 18.
5. Alma Mahler, *My Life, My Loves*, New York: St. Martin's Press, 1989.
6. Karen Monson, *Alma Mahler, Muse to Genius*, Boston: Houghton Mifflin Company, 1983, p. 40.
7. *Ibid.*, p. 43.
8. *Ibid.*, p. XVI.
9. Alma Mahler-Werfel Diaries, The Alma Mahler-Werfel Collection, Special Collections, Van Pelt-Dietrich Library Center, University of Pennsylvania, August 19, 1915.
10. *Ibid.*, September 16, 1915.
11. *Ibid.*, Autumn, 1916.

Special thanks to Tom Lehrer for permission to include his wonderful song in its entirety.

CHAPTER X

JESSICA LANGE

Three-Time Winner (Bob Fosse, Mikhail Baryshnikov, Sam Shepard)

Why, having won her, do I woo?
Because her spirit's vestal grace
Provokes me always to pursue
But, spirit-like, eludes embrace.

—Coventry Patmore,
The Married Lover

SHE'S A PRETTY BLONDE from Minnesota with a slightly crooked nose that comes from smashing into a parking meter when she was a child and a nice figure, but one that at the age of forty-one needs the regimen of exercise and diet to keep it trim. Intelligent and articulate, she speaks with the obsessively introspective, pseudo-psychoanalytical verbiage of the sixties, answering interviewers with phrases such as "inner spirit investigation," "the first foot of self-genesis" and the other terms that cause instant MEGO (journalistic jargon for "mine eyes glaze over").

With no seemingly outstanding qualifications, this woman has accumulated the following brilliant list of lovers: Bob Fosse, the multi-award-winning Broadway and Hollywood dancer/choreographer/director; Mikhail Baryshnikov, the great Russian ballet dancer; and now Sam Shepard, the playwright and actor.

163

Jessica Lange at the New York Film Critics Awards at the Rainbow Room, January 13, 1991. *(Photo by Robin Platzer Twin Images)*

Not only are all these men knockouts in their fields, but the last two are sexy as hell. Baryshnikov with his heavy-lidded gray eyes and wonderfully sinewy dancer's body has drawn a stream of gorgeous women since the day he defected to the United States. They line up at his dressing room and swoon with delight at signs of his favor. His carnal conquests have been covered by the media ad nauseam, but the one woman he says may be the only one he truly loved and with whom he spent six years and who is the mother of his child is Jessica Lange.

Sam Shepard is the epitome of the strong silent type, exuding the sexiness of the unreachable man. His face is lean and weathered, with high cheekbones and brown eyes that slant slightly to give an attractively exotic cast to his face. His brown hair is slightly receding from a widow's peak. He's the rough, tough independent loner whose remote unattainability makes him compelling. Not only is he a fine actor, but also a prolific Pulitzer-Prize-winning playwright. This remarkable renaissance man is not only a hunk, he's a catch. And who got him? Jessica Lange. They live together in unmarried bliss on a farm in Virginia with their two children and Jessica's daughter by Baryshnikov.

Women look at Jessica Lange with puzzlement. She certainly does not seem special in any way. Men, however, react quite differently. There is something about Jessica Lange that evokes in men a sense of their own sexuality; it is her attitude of cool unconcern, concealing an intense inner sensuality and offering men the promise of discovery, that constitutes a particular challenge to successful men. In short, Jessica Lange is the perfect lure for the man who has everything.

Jessica was born in 1950 in Cloquet, Minnesota, a small town near Duluth. Her father, Albert Lange, was a salesman and teacher, a restless man who moved the family from place to place. He is a man whom Jessica describes as "someone who got bored easily." Albert and Jessica's mother, Dorothy, passed on a spirit of independence and restlessness to their children. Sister Anne is a Minneapolis art director who has been living on a sailboat for over fifteen years. Brother George is a commercial pilot. And Jessica, as of 1989, had moved twenty-five times within the past fifteen years.

She entered the University of Minnesota in 1968 on an art scholarship, but according to her, felt trapped and almost suffocated and wanted to get out into the "real world." Her innate restlessness dovetailed perfectly with the philosophy of the sixties. These were the Bob Dylan days and his "Subterranean Homesick Blues" was her anthem. She hung out for a while in the Minneapolis version of Haight-Ashbury known as "Dinkytown," but her real break-out opportunity arrived in the form of a handsome Spanish photographer named Paco Grande. She dropped out of college, to the disapproval of her parents, and she and Paco did their own version of *Easy Rider* in a pickup truck, in which they traveled the country in full flower-child style. They married in 1970, a rite Jessica has never explained or repeated; it was certainly not stylish in her set and didn't fit in with the Soho life they would live in New York.

"It was the sixties and everything was exploding," remembered Jessica in a 1990 article by Linda Bird Francke. "So I ran off with Paco, who was by far the most exotic creature I had ever laid my eyes on. We lived for a while in Europe, then ended up back here living out of the back of a truck. He opened up all sorts of worlds to me through his knowledge of music and literature and art and Europe—all those things that became fascinating to a small-town girl from Minnesota."[1]

They lived for a while in the Soho section of New York City in an illegal unconverted loft in the days before the smart set fell in love with Poor Chic and began deserting their uptown designer apartments for primitive Bowery lofts into which they sank thousands of dollars to transform them into luxurious drop-dead designer replicas of their uptown apartments. Jessica went to Paris and came back. Somewhere

along the way, Paco seemed to drop out of the picture, actually if not legally, and in 1975 Jessica was alone in New
York, supporting herself by waitressing at the Lion's Head, a
Greenwich Village literary hangout. It was the kind of place
in which there was no caste division between patrons and the
hired help and she is remembered as the willowy blonde
with the crooked nose who was unresponsive to the clever
come-ons of the saloon's regulars. Everyone knew a little
about everyone else, though backgrounds were usually ro-
mantically vague and mysterious. It was known that Jessica
was a midwestern girl who had dropped out of college, run
off in her teens to marry a Spanish photographer and live in
Europe, studied as a mime in Paris and become involved in
experimental theatre in Soho. Excellent credentials for the
times. As she usually fended off the locals, they were somewhat offended when a thin, short and somewhat effete
Frenchman picked her up after work one day. They later
learned that he was Philippe Petit, the man who had climbed
to the top of the World Trade Center and performed other
extraordinarily daring feats.

Jessica indulged in the usual round of finding-yourself activities of young women in the sixties: taking classes in acting, dancing, painting (her specialty was painting formica
boxes), even doing a little bit of modeling for the Wilhel-
mina agency. Her study of mime in Paris had an enormous
effect upon her and in many ways helped her later acting
career. She worked with Etienne Decroux, the guru of classi-
cal mime who taught Marcel Marceau, and she speaks of him
today with reverence: "We would work sometimes for weeks
on just the movement of a hand, just from the physical point
of view, getting the technical thing right. Or a movement of
the eyes. And then all of a sudden one morning he'd sweep
in and say, 'You're not gymnasts, you're dramatic artists.'
And then he'd take a movement that had been just physical
for weeks and spin these incredible tales, these incredible
fantasies about it. And it became literature."[2]

She also worked with Ellie Klein, whose very avant-garde dance company outdid Merce Cunningham in starkness and esoteric symbolism. Klein also involved her group in tap dancing, and Jessica found herself dancing with stars of the Dixie Hotel Tap Revue and with greats such as Sandman Sims and Chuck Green.

Jessica was captivated by the freedom and creative excitement to be found in New York in the sixties and now frequently alludes to those days with the loving nostalgia of the ex-flower-children Keaton parents on *Family Ties*. It was a time when underground everythings were forming; people were painting things that had never been painted before in ways that had never been seen; plays were being performed in basements everywhere; dance groups were displaying new techniques and approaches. Nothing was too outrageous; if it was totally off-the-wall and incomprehensible, it was called "experimental." It was a time when anyone who actually had or fancied he had a shred of creativity could play it out in public with total confidence that it would be taken seriously.

Interested in all the performing arts, Jessica was looking for acting parts. She detested auditioning, a feeling she maintains to this day, but there was little choice for aspirants. When she heard that Dino De Laurentiis was undertaking a highly publicized search for an unknown actress to star in *King Kong*, his $24-million epic, she decided to test for the role, figuring it meant a free trip to the coast, and she might be able to see her sister in San Diego. Within a week, she was chosen, signed to a contract, and they were filming the movie.

King Kong was one of the major flops of the decade, and turned out to be one of those embarrassments that comedians and talk-show hosts love to lampoon. Unfortunately, Jessica became part of the big joke and she saw her film career suddenly headed for oblivion. It's tough to be taken seriously as an actress when you're known everywhere as King Kong's girlfriend, an epithet that dogged her for years. But one of the advantages of starring in a film, no matter how disastrous, is that you do get seen and maybe, if you're lucky, by an important person who sees something in you. In Jessica's case, it was Bob Fosse.

"When I would talk about her after *King Kong*, people's eyes would sort of glaze over," Bob Fosse said. "There's a strong prejudice in Hollywood against someone in a picture that wasn't a big success. But I thought she was wonderful in it. Other than being so beautiful, she was very funny."

Bob Fosse's reaction was highly personal. In the dictionary, "beautiful" is defined as "what stirs a heightened response of the senses and the mind on its highest level." And obviously, as their future relationship proved, she definitely stirred his senses. He wrote to her praising her performance and their romance began.

Robert Louis Fosse was barely out of his teens when Hollywood started to tout him as the next Astaire. He was a magnificent dancer, although the highly stylized coiled tension and manic strut that became the hallmark of his dancing and of his tremendous body of choreographic work could not have been further from Astaire's easy, relaxing, loping style.

He loved to perform, but his major talent lay in staging. Before he reached thirty, he had won two successive Tony awards for his choreography of *The Pajama Game* in 1955 and *Damn Yankees* in 1956. During his lifetime he accumulated ten Tony awards, and in 1973 achieved the unmatched feat of winning an Oscar, a Tony and an Emmy in a single year for directing the movie *Cabaret*, Broadway's big hit, *Pippin*, and the Liza Minnelli TV special, *Liza with a Z*.

Fosse was a multitalented genius who was highly respected on both coasts. In 1974, while simultaneously editing the film *Lenny* and rehearsing the Broadway musical *Chicago*, he suffered a massive heart attack. He gave up cocaine and uppers and cut down on drinking. "I am an addictive personality," he admitted, but continued to smoke, overplay and overwork. He drove his friends crazy by sticking to his diet rigidly when ordering food in a restaurant while urging companions to order delicious high-cholesterol items —and then eating liberally off their plates.

At the time he met Jessica, he was working on the movie *All That Jazz*, a portrayal of his own experiences, frequently referred to as the world's first and probably only open-heart musical. The movie ended with his character's death staged as a major production number.

Bob Fosse's letter to Jessica was, as she put it, the only positive thing that emerged from the *King Kong* debacle. At the time their relationship began, he was just starting to work on *All That Jazz*, and Jessica loved the auteur tone of the script. He offered to write a small part for her, that of Angelique, the seductive angel of death. It had been two years since *King Kong* and she felt she could use the exposure. The studio brass were against her participation because they saw it as merely a token of Fosse's casting-couch quid pro quo and regarded this Lange girl as just another of those vapid faces over good bodies who hang around Hollywood until it's time to return home to marry the local car dealer. The film won nine Oscar nominations, but Jessica's parading around in white gauze uttering a few cryptic lines did little to diminish the dumb blonde image of King Kong's girlfriend.

Then one night Jessica was invited to a Hollywood party at Buck Henry's house, and Milos Forman introduced her to Mikhail Baryshnikov, who was not only the greatest male dancer in the world but the highest paid and, thanks to the film *The Turning Point*, well on his way to becoming a movie idol. There was an instant attraction, which was not unusual for Misha. A man who adores women and views life as a series of romances, he revels in the challenge of making beautiful women fall in love with him and has no difficulty in doing so. As famed dancer-choreographer Twyla Tharp says, "Misha is very attractive. He doesn't put it on; he just IS attractive."[3] At the time he and Jessica met, the media loved him; his personality generated excitement. A May 8, 1978, *New York* magazine article referred to the "overripe look" of his gray eyes and said they "hint[ed] at unreported nighttime activities." He complained that his career kept him too busy to keep up the wild pace the press ascribed to him and that if he had slept with all the women they hinted at, he wouldn't have the strength left for all those jetés. He did admit that he loved to be loved and loved to be in love, and like many writers and artists, believed in the inspirational power of desire.

Jessica was mentioned in the gossip columns as the latest conquest of the romantic Russian. The accepted wisdom was that this was just another of Misha's madcap amours with a dumb blonde starlet looking to take the fuck-the-famous route out of obscurity. But it soon became apparent that neither one of them fit the cliché and that the brooding Russian had found a woman with whom he was deeply in love.

Mikhail Nikolayevich Baryshnikov was born on January 27, 1949, in Riga, Latvia. His father, Nikolai, was a Soviet army officer, a rigid Stalinist who taught military topography. Misha grew up, in a sense, as a foreigner, because he was Russian and all his friends were Latvians; they spoke a different language and even dressed differently. His father was a narrow nationalist who hated Jews and Latvians, which made it difficult for Misha, as most of his friends were one or the other or both, and he never brought friends home for fear his father would insult them. His mother was an unschooled, simple woman who loved opera and theatre and it was she who introduced young Misha to ballet. His father was a remote, unreachable man but he loved his mother deeply.

When he was eleven years old, Misha came home one day to be told, "Mommy died." He later learned she had hanged herself. This is a subject he rarely touches upon today. His father remarried, and young Misha, who was good at folk dancing and soccer but terrible in school, decided to take the exam for the famous Riga State Choreographic School. He passed.

From that point on, his life took on a shape and direction of its own, driven by his instantly apparent talent. By the time he was fifteen, he had moved on to Leningrad into the hands of the famous ballet teacher Alexander Pushkin, who took Baryshnikov on as his new protégé to replace his illustrious famous pupil, Rudolf Nureyev, who had just defected to the West. By 1970 Misha was a leading dancer of the Kirov Ballet. He was sent to London to perform and for the first time was exposed to American musicals and jazz.

On the evening of June 29, 1974, after a stunning performance with the Bolshoi Ballet in Toronto, Misha exited the stage door and, instead of walking toward the KGB-chauffeured car awaiting outside, plunged into the crowd of enthusiastic autograph-seeking fans and headed to a nearby restaurant in which Canadian friends were waiting to whisk him away to a safe house and defection. On July 27, he debuted in New York with the famed defector Soviet ballerina Natalia Makarova in *Giselle*, and a stunned audience gave him a thirty-minute ovation. The effortlessness of his swelling jumps and turns, his flamboyant vitality and brio were utterly dazzling. New York and soon the entire world went wild over this phenomenal, incomparable artist.

At the time he and Jessica met, Baryshnikov was one of the most famous stars in the world and she was a struggling nobody. The outward perception of their affair was that she was merely a tagalong living a derivative existence. This was totally untrue, a role Jessica would never assume. "It angers me when I run into women who are totally submissive, completely dependent," she once said. "What angers me more are men who like that kind of woman." While their careers were in this skewed top-bottom position, it was inevitable that Jessica would be embarrassed by situations such as the one she described angrily to Julia Cameron in an interview for *American Film* magazine: "This man leaned across me and said to Misha, 'I see you travel with your secretary.' "

Their relationship could not involve too much together-ness, which suited both of them. Misha was flying all over the world choreographing and performing, and another woman might have complained, demanded or been just plain misera-ble with a lover whose priorities obviously relegated her to second place. Not so Jessica.

The quality of Jessica Lange that makes her particularly alluring to high-powered men is that she does not want their undivided attention. She does not demand their full-time dedication. She is uncomfortable with that kind of devotion, as it involves a reciprocal responsibility she is unwilling to undertake. Her whole restless history is testimony to the fact that she avoids commitments. She has the need to maintain a slight distance between herself and others and to keep a part of herself private. "I always felt there was something I didn't know about her," said Bob Fosse.

This slight remoteness makes it easy for men whose com-pelling careers would conflict with the needs of a doting lover and absolves them of any possible guilt. The flip side presents the men with the niggling awareness of her mild disinterest, and that is the challenge that creates excitement and stimulation. There is a core of Jessica Lange that every man wants to reach. It is that elusive element that draws men who have always found it easy to win any woman they want; they have finally met the woman who is unattainable, even to them.

The relationship suited Misha well, as closeness and com-mitment were something he carefully eschewed, perhaps due to the traumatic legacy of his mother's death. When an eleven-year-old boy is presented with his mother's suicide, he can see it only two ways: "Why didn't she love me enough to want to stay alive and take care of me?" or "What did I do to make her abandon me?" It is very difficult for him to ever love again, as he only sees love as ending in either his failure or her desertion or both.

During all these years, Jessica was auditioning, doing screen tests for specific parts, the usual pursuits of the starlet in search of success. One of the tests was with Jack Nicholson for a part she did not get in *Going South*. But Jack remembered the test and Jessica.

Bob Rafelson's *Five Easy Pieces* had made a star of Jack Nicholson in 1970. Eleven years later, the two friends were about to do a remake of *The Postman Always Rings Twice*, James M. Cain's steamy book that had been made into a movie in 1946 starring Lana Turner and John Garfield. The book, published in 1934, became instantly infamous and was banned in Boston, of course, and Canada as well. It was a sordid Depression tale of a crude drifter's affair with an immigrant's wife and their plot to murder her husband. The old Hollywood morality and the repressive Hays Office prevented the Turner-Garfield movie from portraying the raw sexuality of the book, and now Rafelson and Nicholson were intent on redoing the tame old version, taking full advantage of the explicit sex permitted these days. The problem was making Jack Nicholson come across as sexy. Rafelson remembered Jessica's test with Jack and noted that Nicholson's reactions to her brought out the side of him that they were seeking. He decided to check her out himself and flew down to South Carolina, where Jessica was working in summer stock.

"We sat in her motel room, and talked, and I found her very interesting," Rafelson said. "She got a phone call around midnight. I asked if she wanted me to leave, but she said no, and I watched her as she stayed on the phone for a half hour. There was something about the girl that was extremely poised. Her posture on the bed while she was talking made her seem like an incredibly sensual lady."

There are a few points in this tale that are noteworthy. Who stays on the phone for a half hour while entertaining a guest? This wasn't a guy selling vacuum cleaners but an important man who could provide the career break of a lifetime. It's not only rude, inconsiderate and awkward, but imprudent. Or deliberate. If the conversation goes on that long, it's apparently personal. Why would Jessica have wanted to discuss intimate details with an audience? As a matter of fact, the phone call was one of Misha's keeping-in-touch calls that characterized much of their long-distance relationship, so there had to be some lovey talk. This was a small motel room, not a suite, so Rafelson was forced to listen—and watch.

There is nothing in Jessica's history that indicates she is either unintelligent or ill-bred. The only interpretation of her odd behavior is that she was auditioning, and the phone call was a part of her performance. Remember Luise Rainer's Academy Award-winning rendition of a heartbreaking phone call in *The Great Ziegfeld*? It is amazing how much can be conveyed by facial expressions and body language as one lies sprawled across a bed, virtually caressing the phone. Rafelson probably had to duck under a cold shower the moment he left Jessica's room.

He was impressed, but obviously felt he needed more convincing evidence of Jessica's suitability for the lead in what was undoubtedly going to be a major film. He flew her out to the coast and videotaped her in a number of more intimate scenes, you know, just to see if she was really right for the role. Apparently Rafelson was loath to bother Nicholson by asking him to work with Jessica in these taxing tests, so he conserved his friend's energy by playing the male part himself. What are friends for? Obviously Rafelson is a very particular guy because he interviewed and tested over one hundred other actresses; the man's a glutton for work. But in the end, perfectionist Rafelson came back to Jessica.

Here was the woman who better than anyone else could turn on Jack Nicholson. He says that acting with her helped him increase his own sexuality. He says she's like a delicate fawn crossed with a Buick. He says all men drop at her feet. He says she has rolling midwestern female sensuality. Do you get the idea?

From all I have read about on-location filming, it becomes a totally encapsulated world for the participants in which The Work, as they call it, becomes their current reality and the real world lies somewhere far away. With a movie like *The Postman Always Rings Twice*, which features the graphic depiction of a sordid sexual relationship between two primitives— well, this must have been some X-rated on-set world. The steamy outtakes from the film are still part of Hollywood legend.

Jack Nicholson explained what he perceived as the mandatory ambience for fostering creativity in such a film: "To open up the area of erotic acting, we had to establish some kind of on-set society. . . . I didn't want to be holding back, and yet I didn't want Jessica to feel like she had to lock herself in at night for fear I'd be crawling naked through her window, a sex maniac or something."[4]

You get the sense that an open permissiveness that allowed free expression of sexual feelings at all times was established on the set under the heading of being essential to The Work. After all, we don't want any repression that has to be overcome for the cameras. Jessica was grateful to Rafelson for creating a pressure-free environment by giving over the set to her and Jack for as long as they needed it to prepare for the famous screwing-her-to-the-kitchen-table scene. Jack was especially grateful, but more so to Jessica: "What I loved about Jessica is that, like Ginger Rogers made Fred Astaire more sexual, Jessica made me look good as a partner."[5]

That's like the conversational gambit of the egotist who says, "Enough of this talk about me, let's talk about you. What do YOU think of ME?"

Somehow it's hard to think of Jack Nicholson being insecure about anything, but the inevitable picture to be drawn from all this concern for the proper showcasing of his sexual-

JESSICA LANGE 177

ity is of a guy who is uncertain of his performance in at least one area.

Rafelson and Nicholson have described how at times they had to deliberately provoke Jessica before a scene in order to get the best performance from her. They took her for long walks in order to get her so tired that she forgot to be nervous; they called her obscene names to goad her into the anger the director needed for the next take. They do not make it sound as though Jessica Lange is a natural actress.

Although *The Postman Always Rings Twice* got mixed reviews, Jessica was praised, and once and for all was able to shed the onus of *King Kong*. The controversial film was unquestionably a landmark movie, not only for Jessica but, more importantly, for the way it allowed sex to be depicted in American films. It was not greeted with wild success in this country, doing far better in Europe, possibly because Europeans have always been less self-conscious about sexuality.

At last Jessica had achieved her goal of being regarded as a serious actress and her career position relative to the famous Misha's was now no longer so lopsided; she had achieved star status and was being besieged with offers. Just at that time, at age thirty-one, Jessica learned she was pregnant with thirty-two-year-old Misha's child.

Jessica was delighted; Misha gave the situation mixed reviews. Both decided she would have the child, but there was no talk of marriage. For one thing, she was not yet divorced, and secondly, neither saw any reason for a wedding.

On March 5, 1981, Jessica felt twinges, and as it was a nice, gently snowy day in New York, she walked twenty blocks to the doctor's office. When he reassured her that she wasn't having contractions, she walked the twenty blocks home. As she walked in the door, she went into labor and two hours later gave birth to an eight-pound baby girl. It all happened so fast that she did not even have time to call Misha, who was touring with his company in Buffalo, New York. When he did get the news, he flew home immediately and was delirious with delight to behold his daughter, whom they called Alexandra after his mother, a name shortened in Russian to Shura.

This began a totally new life for Jessica and Misha. The two restless rovers suddenly had a mutual mooring, a focus to their lives, and for the first time, someone who was more important than they. Domesticity became important, and Jessica moved twenty-eight blocks uptown into Misha's large Park Avenue apartment. During that first summer, they searched for a weekend and summer home. In Sneden's Landing, a lovely spot conveniently situated just thirty minutes north of New York City, they found a turn-of-the-century converted barn amidst five tree-and fern-covered acres on a bluff overlooking the scenic Hudson River. Their neighbors down the road were Al Pacino and Ellen Burstyn.

Misha adored his daughter and was very much in love with Jessica. Life was lovely, but there must be the dance. That winter, when Shura was not yet a year old, Misha went off on tour and Jessica went off with the baby to a rented house in Los Angeles, a city she hated. However, she had finally been given the role of her career, the role she had been preparing for for years—that of the star-crossed actress Frances Farmer.

Jessica had always been fascinated with the tragic life of the beautiful blonde thirties star who had been a victim of Hollywood and the psychiatric establishment. During her New York years, she had done a great deal of research on the actress's life and seemed to feel there was some sort of cosmic connection between them. She desperately wanted to play the lead in the bio-flick that was to be made under the title of *Frances*. It was considered a hot role, and she vied with Sissy Spacek, Meryl Streep, Diane Keaton, Jane Fonda, Goldie Hawn and Tuesday Weld for the juicy plum. When she won out, Jessica arranged her life around preparing herself for the part. She and Shura moved into their house, and Jessica began spending hours in the gym to shed postnatal weight, working ten hours a week with an acting coach, read-

ing everything that had been written by and about Farmer
and screening all her films over and over again.

Frances was a major turning point for Jessica Lange. The
filming was an emotionally draining experience that required
the maintenance of a level of passion and rage that ultimately
deteriorated into despair and death. It is difficult to turn such
intensity on and off. Sam Shepard played her boyfriend in
the film, and soon life mirrored fiction and they began a
torrid affair.

Frances made Jessica a star; it also ended her alliance with
Misha. After filming was finished, she took Shura and went
to Minnesota, where she had built a log cabin with no phone
or television on 122 acres of land, including a stocked trout
stream, near her parents' home. She had finalized her divorce from Paco Grande after long and costly legal battles
and after paying him reputedly a rather hefty settlement.
Misha talked of marriage. They had been apart all winter,
and he told the press that his family was now his main joy.
But his busy career meant a life of long-distance communication, and Jessica was talking about raising a family, the bond-
ing of the generations and the creation of a somewhat normal life for her daughter. Then Sam came along.

Samuel Shepard Rogers VII was born on November 5,
1943, in Fort Sheridan, Illinois, and was given the name his
forebears had used for six generations. His father was a career army officer, which meant the family moved around the
country many times during Sam's childhood. When his father retired after putting in his twenty years, the family finally settled down on an avocado-growing sheep ranch in
Duarte, California. The livelihood produced by the ranch
was precarious, but Sam loved working with the soil and
with animals, interests that stayed with him. Influenced by his
father's interest in Dixieland jazz, Sam learned to play the
drums and began what became a lifetime involvement with
rock 'n' roll and jazz and its subculture.

Like many other famous writers, Sam did not shine in

school. His sole stab at advanced education was a one-year stint studying agricultural science at the local Mount Antonio Junior College. Meanwhile back at the ranch, the bucolic peace was being destroyed by his father's alcoholism. Sam escaped the hysterical family scene by joining a touring theatrical group, which finally landed him, at age nineteen, in New York City as one of the army of aspiring actors struggling to survive while awaiting their big breaks.

He ran into an old high school friend, Charlie Mingus, Jr., son of the famous jazz musician, who got Sam a job at the Village Gate nightclub and soon involved him in the same exhilarating explosion of cultural freedom that so affected Jessica Lange. An off-off Broadway company named Theatre Genesis needed plays, so Sam decided to take a shot and knocked off two one-acters called *Cowboy* and *The Rock Garden*. Most of the critics called them bad imitations of Beckett, but the *Village Voice* loved them. Sam began to churn out more one-act plays and soon developed a cult following. *Newsweek* critic Jack Kroll was impressed with the personal stream-of-consciousness style of these early plays: "The true artist starts with his obsessions, then makes them ours as well," he wrote. "The very young Sam Shepard exploded his obsessions like firecrackers; in his crazy, brilliant early plays he was escaping his demons, not speaking to ours."[6]

In 1970 Sam hit the big time with the production of his *Operation Sidewinder* at Lincoln Center's Vivian Beaumont Theatre and was recognized as a major playwright. The year before, he had married actress O-Lan Johnson and they had had a son, Jesse Mojo.

Shepard had been experimenting with drugs heavily as well as drinking to excess. In the hope that distancing himself and his family from the jazz and rock world of heavy substance abuse might help him kick all the madness, he took his wife and son and moved to London. He wrote some of his finest works while in England, and was courted by both Broadway and Hollywood. Sam could now write his own ticket, and he decided to put himself in front of the camera as well as behind it. After directing his 1983 play *Fool for Love*, he played the starring role in the movie version, and since 1978 has taken enough roles to become a matinee-idol celebrity.

Shepard is one of those multitalented people against whom one should not try to measure himself for fear of sinking into utter despair. He is great at everything, amazingly prolific and marvelous looking. He has written thirty-seven plays, three books, and a number of screenplays, has won eleven Obie awards for best off-Broadway plays, one National Institute and American Academy award for literature, the New York Drama Critics' Circle award for *A Lie of the Mind* and the Pulitzer Prize for drama in 1979 for *Buried Child*. As if that weren't enough, he received an Academy Award nomination for best supporting actor in *The Right Stuff*. Have I mentioned that he plays drums and guitar with rock groups and has been called by Jack Kroll "the poet laureate of America's emotional badlands"?

Sam Shepard's marriage to O-Lan Johnson was one of those long marriages with intermittent time-outs, such as the time he went off with Patti Smith, with whom he wrote the play *Cowboy Mouth*. But, as the gossip columnists commented approvingly, he always came back home to his wife and son.

But not forever. In 1984 he, Jessica and Shura moved into the ranch they had bought in Santa Fe and proceeded to become a family. They chose New Mexico because both wanted to be as far removed from Hollywood as possible and both love horses. He competes in rodeos and plays polo, and Jessica jumps. They now have a daughter, Hannah Jane, and a son, Samuel Walker, and although Sam is now divorced, do not consider marriage a necessity. In 1988 they decided to move even further away from Hollywood and bought a farm in Virginia, where, at last visit, they are very much in love and thriving in happy domestic bliss.

Unlike the long-distance relationship with Misha, Jessica

now has a man who shares her home life and also shares her
work life. They starred together in the film *Country*, and he
wrote the movie *Far North* when she asked him to create a
vehicle for her when she was pregnant with their second
child. There are definite advantages for an actress with a live-
in playwright, as Mia Farrow can attest. From all reports, Sam
and Jessica are doing just fine.

Of course, Misha and O-Lan might not be feeling too wonderful, but that's show biz. Both Baryshnikov and Jessica
Lange have made statements about their acceptance of the
transitory quality of relationships. Her words were to the
effect that Hell, I work all day, I don't need to come home
and work on a relationship. When the emotional high is
gone, it's time to quit. That sounds reasonable, but what
happens when only one of the couple is ready to abort?
Where does that leave the dumpee? Jessica's defection left
Misha in deep desolation. He told a *Rolling Stone* interviewer
that it took him a few years to get over it and that he still
loves her and will always be saddened by the separation.
"It's a big regret that will be with me for the rest of my
life."[7] Of course, he speaks nobly about being happy for her,
and evinces understanding of her new needs and how his
failures contributed to the breakup, but he was still pretty
angry when, shortly after the split, little Shura slipped one
day and called him "Sam."

It seems strange that a man who has made a career of
romances and relationships should be so hard hit by this one
failure, so much so that, even today, it is a rare interview in
which the subject does not come up. This is certainly a tribute to the powerful allure of Jessica Lange, but even more to
his connection of her desertion with the suicide of his
mother.

Misha's flamboyant behavior with women before Jessica
was the mark of a man who feared closeness. Who could
blame him? The one deep love he had with a woman ended
in her cruelly abandoning him. But then came Jessica, and

even though he obviously loved her deeply, he deferred commitment. The arrival of their daughter, however, changed everything, because suddenly there was the configuration of a family—mother, father and child—and he was back in the warmth of his early childhood. It was the most wonderful time of his life, as he tells it, and he started to let his defenses down and talk about marriage. Then Jessica stopped loving him and took it all away—the love, the home, the family—and he was once again left alone and abandoned. The pain of the desertion is apparently still there and has undoubtedly reinforced his distrust of relationships.

Jessica Lange herself is not the greatest believer in permanence either, which is part of her charm to men, but they had better be ready for the downside. She is a restless woman who has her own version of stability. She has put down roots with Sam Shepard and has lived with him and their children in the most conventional domesticity for seven years but sees no reason to marry. When asked about this, she answered heatedly: "I think marriage is about your commitment to the other person. It has absolutely nothing to do with a government decree. The legality of it means absolutely nothing to me whatsoever. That's not going to make people live their lives together and be responsible to each other."[8]

Earlier in the same article she attacks the American attitude toward marriage as a sign of national weakness. "I think that's what's wrong with America—the family's becoming disposable. You know, if you don't like your wife, you can get rid of her; if you don't like your husband for a day, you can get rid of him." She sees the impending disintegration of the family unit as "a signal of the end, of this whole kind of apocalyptic feeling that is in the air now."[9]

The only possible way to reconcile those two statements is to assume that her view of domestic permanence is parents and children all living together for a steady period—seven years at least. But she is unwilling to sign on for the long haul with any man because who knows what's coming up next. It's that elusive quality, the realization that Jessica's sense of permanence can change at any time that makes her so satisfying and tantalizing to powerful men.

We see what draws such men to Jessica, but what need directs Jessica toward geniuses? All women find such men desirable and fascinating, but she apparently has the compulsion and drive to capture them. Unlike Mia Farrow and Alma Mahler, who openly averred that they were only interested in great men, she has never made any public statement indicating that these are the only kinds of males she considers acceptable partners. But like Mia, Alma and Françoise, she has a strong father, difficult to please, whose approval she seeks and will probably never get. "One of the most important motivating factors in my entire life has been trying to please my father," she has said. "Because he is an amazing man, unbelievably powerful in his personality and magnetic and riveting. And polarizing. I loved him and hated him. But I always, always, needed his approval, and it was hard to get. It still is hard to get."[10]

Like Alma's, Mia's, and Françoise's fathers, Albert Lange is not one of your world-class greats, but in his daughter's eyes, he is an incomparable man. How, then, could Jessica settle for anything less, and how better can she prove her value than by bringing home a genius or two? Listen, Daddy, you may not think I'm so hot, but look at these brilliant guys who do. Maybe it's time for you to revise my rating.

With that compulsive star-search motivation, permanence can only be a temporary illusion. When asked what made her and Sam move from New Mexico all the way to Virginia, she answered: "We were living in New Mexico until two years ago and somehow it just didn't feel right to me. You know you can feel when you're meant to be in some place and then you know your time there is past. And it's time to move on."[11]

If I were Sam Shepard, I wouldn't count on sharing my social security checks with Jessica.

References

1. "The Enigmatic Allure of Jessica Lange," Linda Bird Francke, *Interview,* December 1989.
2. "Jessica Lange Sex and Subtext," Ron Rosenbaum, *Vanity Fair*, October 1988.
3. "Misha," Arthur Gold and Robert Fizdale, *Vanity Fair*, January 1987.
4. Rosenbaum, *op. cit.*
5. *Ibid.*
6. Contemporary Authors, New Revision Series, Gale Research Co., Detroit, Michigan, 1988, Volume 22, p. 424.
7. N. Collins, *Rolling Stone*, October 8, 1987, p. 56.
8. Rosenbaum, *op. cit.*
9. *Ibid.*
10. *Ibid.*
11. *Ibid.*

CHAPTER XI

WALLY SIMPSON

The Iron Duchess

*Woman would be more charming if one could fall into
her arms without falling into her hands.*
— Ambrose Bierce,
Epigrams

BEAUTIFUL? FORGET IT. Charming? Sometimes. Brilliant?
Are you kidding? Sexy? If you like making it with coat hangers.

QUESTION: Then what on earth did this bony Baltimore
double-divorcée have that enabled her to snare the most eligible man in the world, the king of England?

ANSWER: She had the acuity to recognize that her neurosis dovetailed perfectly with his neurosis and the two of them
were ideally suited to live unhappily ever after.

Wallis Warfield Spencer Simpson was a woman determined
to dominate, and Prince Edward Albert Christian George
Andrew Patrick David was an insecure man who sought to
be subjugated in order to fulfill the degraded self-image instilled in him by a tyrannical father and a cold mother.

This, of course, is an oversimplified explanation. There is
no doubt that Wallis possessed the standard equipment to
attract and manipulate a man with the neurotic needs of the

187

Wally Simpson (Duchess of Windsor) 1936. *(AP/World Wide Photos)*

prince. But the actual conquest was far more complicated and demanded all the inherent abilities and developed skills of this daughter of a poor relative of a wealthy Baltimore family.

Bessie Wallis Warfield was born on June 19, 1896, to Teackle Wallis Warfield and Alys Montague, both members of patrician American families who had met and married at a tuberculosis sanitarium in the Blue Ridge Mountains to which they had both come for treatment. Alys's case was apparently mild and she was shortly cured, but Teackle's condition worsened and he died at age twenty-seven, leaving a penniless widow and five-month-old daughter. Thus Bessie Wallis (soon shortened to Wallis) grew up on the fringes of wealth, forever in the unenviable position of the needy relative of a well-to-do family.

Although it's hard for those of us who live meat-and-potato lives to agonize for the poor young girl whose uncle and aunt refused to subsidize debutante balls and tea dances in her honor and thus deprived her of what she saw as her due, to Wallis these disappointments and deprivations were seminal. She was born with an indestructible belief in self and an unwavering sense of entitlement. Her mother often quoted Wallis's childhood expression "must-have, got-to-get." She saw the world in terms of her needs and her only miscalculations in life came from the erroneous assumption that everyone else would perform accordingly. How could wealthy Uncle Sol (Solomon Davies Warfield) refuse to give her a coming-out ball just because it was 1914 and thousands of young men were being slaughtered in Europe in the Great War? How could the English government insist that King Edward abdicate rather than accept her as his wife?

A psychiatrist friend of mine once explained his own despotic behavior and lengthy list of personal demands with the calm, simple statement, "My needs are greater than those of most people." Like Wallis, he had the blind certainty that he was sui generis, and was surprised rather than angry when people disappointed him. Failure was never his fault, but rather the fault of those around him.

Such people are authoritative and assertive because it is easy to make decisions when you are not confused by self-doubt or burdened with the need to consider the concerns of others. While she was sitting for photographer Cecil Beaton, Wallis said that she was like a man in many ways. "I had a surer idea of what I wanted than most women do, and so had little trouble in making up my mind."[1]

How enchanting and enviable such strong single-mindedness must have seemed to a man who had spent his childhood being disparaged by a martinet father who subscribed to the school of destructive criticism, and whose self-confidence had been further eroded by a cold, dispassionate mother who believed in discipline rather than affection?

In his book *A King's Story*, the Duke of Windsor describes an upbringing that would make child psychologists blanch. The royal family's idea of instilling character in a boy being groomed to take over the reins of the empire shows not only appalling ignorance, but a heartless lack of concern for the child's needs. "If through my family's position my childhood was spared the mundane struggle that is the common lot, I nevertheless had my full share of discipline," he wrote. "For the concept of duty was drilled into me and I never had the sense that the days belonged to me alone."[2]

It has been said that a man who has his father's approval will grow up with unassailable self-confidence. Certainly the converse seems to be true; witness the number of books and plays written about the diminished state of men who go through life scarred by their continuously unsuccessful appeals for signs of parental love and approbation. The October 14, 1990, issue of *The New York Times Magazine* described the emergence of a rapidly growing men's movement proposing that men suffer terrible grief from the wounds inflicted on them by their fathers. "Men feel a sense of loss that their fathers were never the kind of fathers they wished them to be, or needed. . . . Fathers have shamed us and criticized us."[3] The pathetic picture that emerges from the duke's book is that of a father-son relationship based on fear rather than feeling, in which the only communication was reprimands. Even when David was a grown man, his father submitted him to constant humiliation. As Alden Hatch described in *The Mountbattens*, "A palace official heard [George IV] giving his son a dressing-down. In his best storm-at-sea voice, the old king roared, 'You dress like a cad. You act like a cad. You *are* a cad. Get out!' " The prince loved his mother more than his father, but he was terrified of them both.

"I have often felt that despite his undoubted affection for all of us, my father preferred children in the abstract and that his notion of a small boy's place in a grown-up world was summed up in the phrase 'Children should be seen and not heard,' " he wrote.

"It was once said of him that his naval training had caused him to look upon his own children much as he regarded noisy midshipmen when he was the captain of a British cruiser—as young nuisances in constant need of correction. No words that I was ever to hear could be so disconcerting to the spirit as the summons, usually delivered by a footman, that 'His Royal Highness wishes to see you in the library.' My father's study was in a sense his 'Captain's Cabin,' and one never knew on being summoned there what one might be in for . . . more often we would be called to account for some alleged act of misbehavior . . . so the library became for us the seat of parental authority, the place of admonition and reproof."[4]

To compound his difficulties further, the prince was a totally mediocre man. He was of only average intelligence, if that, and was a poor student, a fact that should not have surprised his parents, as the family line offered little genetic promise for braininess. Their handling of his scholastic deficiencies underscored their own poor judgment: instead of building the young prince's self-confidence with encouragement or changing his tutorial arrangements, they told him he was stupid, thereby inevitably creating a self-fulfilling prophecy.

"Our apparent lack of progress under Mr. Hansell, our tutor, used to worry my mother; she blamed him for not arousing in us the spark of ambition to learn, which she was sure lay dormant in Bertie's character and mine," the Duke of Windsor recalled. "My father, however, took the opposite view. Defending Mr. Hansell's method, he maintained with disheartening candor that the fault lay in my dumbness."[5]

When he attended the Royal Naval College, he was not far from the bottom of the class and his grades continued to be poor. Unfortunately, he could not compensate for his lack of scholarship by performing well in athletics, the other measurement of a young English gentleman's value. He possessed little aptitude for football, cricket, hockey, even horsemanship: "My father saw me riding and suddenly discovered that my seat on a horse—an indispensable accomplishment for princes in those days—left much to be desired. From then on he was constantly finding fault with me on this score. But to no avail; I just did not like riding."[6] All in all, he was a very ordinary man who was constantly made aware of his lackluster abilities by a father who continued to point out his deficiencies.

It is interesting to learn that in later years, after the death of his father, he came to enjoy riding and it became a principal source of pleasure to him. Another activity he picked up in childhood and enjoyed for the rest of his life was crocheting, hardly the sort of manly activity designated to please his father, whose idea of a great day was December 18, 1913, when he personally shot over 1,000 pheasants in an outing at the home of Lord Burnham (the total number slaughtered came to almost 4,000 birds).

Despite the disparagement he received at home, David's public image as Prince of Wales was that of a man whose destiny would someday bring him to the throne of the British Empire, who would control personal wealth almost beyond belief. Single, handsome, he was the catch of the century. Surely such a man should have been the most secure, self-important, contented man in the world.

But Wallis Warfield Spencer Simpson shrewdly saw through the regal facade. Having married two weak men, she could spot another at ten paces and knew exactly how to handle such an individual. Although neither brilliant nor beautiful, she was magnificently secure in her ability to attract men. Her now-famous opening line when she first met him is a testimony to her shrewdness. As the story goes, they met at a weekend party in one of the stately homes so famous in England for their magnificent architecture and appalling amenities. As usual, it was cold, damp and foggy and Mrs. Simpson was suffering from a severe head cold.

As he recounts in his book, "Since a prince is by custom expected to take the lead in conversing with strangers, and having been informed that she was an American, I was prompted to observe that she must miss central heating, of which there was a lamentable lack in my country and an abundance in hers. The affirmative answer that, under the circumstances, any Briton had reason to expect would then have cleared the way for a casual discussion of the variety of physical comforts available in America, and the conversation would have been safely anchored on firm ground. Instead a verbal chasm opened under my feet. Mrs. Simpson did not miss the great boon that her country has conferred upon the world. On the contrary, she liked the cold houses of Great Britain. A mocking look came into her eyes. 'I am sorry, Sir,' she said, 'but you have disappointed me.'

" 'In what way?' "

" 'Every American woman who comes to your country is always asked that same question. I had hoped for something more original from the Prince of Wales.'

"I moved away to talk to the other guests, but the echoes of the passage lingered."[7]

Now is that a clever opening gambit to intrigue the prince, or what? In just three sentences, she put him right back in his father's library at the scene of his most soul-searing life encounters, back to the familiar ground of failure and unfulfilled expectations. "You disappoint me" was a line calculated to reach that raw spot of love-hate relationship with the father whom he could never seem to please. In her initial exchange with the prince, the not-gorgeous not-anything woman from Baltimore skillfully managed to press all his buttons and make an indelible impression on the vulnerable future monarch.

How much more effective and memorable an introduction than some inane banter about plumbing and the weather. The conversation was so on the mark that one must wonder if it was planned rather than spontaneous. After all, it was easy for Wallis to do her homework. Knowing the prince would be there, it wouldn't have been difficult to quiz her smart friends about the prince's propensities. It was known that he was both afraid and resentful of his father's domination. The old king's constant berating had undermined him so thoroughly that he had the strength of character of a mound of Jell-O and was known to be highly suggestible. It was said of him that he reset his watch by every clock that he passed. The British Empire Exhibition at Wembley in 1924 displayed a statue of the prince modeled in butter; the medium proved symbolic.

Apparently, the American/Briton conversational cliché in aristocratic social circles, where originality was never prized, was the one about England's lack of central heating, a factor the English seem to regard proudly as a sign of strong national character and others view as indicative of the stolid complacency that lost them the empire. Wallis knew she could anticipate the usual ice-breaking inanities from the less-than-creative prince and prepared her riposte accordingly. It was just the kind of planning that could be expected from a woman like Wallis.

Wallis was also prepared—and had been for quite some time—to deal with the problem of her less-than-stunning looks. The handicap of being born beautiful is that it stunts the development of character and charm: why bother when the first glance wows them? Wallis was completely aware of her physical shortcomings, but given the superb self-confidence with which she was born, she regarded her defects not as drawbacks but as factors to be handled.

"I had an idea that I was the siren type," she once said, "so I mustn't dress like other girls. I must dress differently, in an exotic way. Slinky. Vampish. You know, something tighter or looser, whichever 'they' weren't wearing."[8]

When Jerome Zerbe, the society photographer, took pictures of her in Palm Beach in 1948, she matter-of-factly told him to pick out the ones that made her look least like a horse. Her total lack of beauty was frequently commented upon.

Cecil Beaton said, "I never saw a portrait that looked like her. She's very difficult to draw and paint. I'm usually excellent at catching a likeness, but I once spent a whole afternoon with her and failed. In her news photo, the light strikes the tip of her rather bulbous nose. None of her features is classically correct, her nose, for instance; and her mouth is downright ugly, but they all fit together. She's attractively ugly, *une belle laide*. She has an amusing face."[9]

With the creative initiative that she always exhibited, Wallis distracted attention from her deficiencies by being outstandingly chic, razor thin, a graceful dancer and assiduously au courant so that she could converse intelligently. And always, she carried herself magnificently.

She has been described by friends and acquaintances as one who was filled with "pep," who "was wonderful company," who "shone at parties," all traits characteristic of an individual consciously evolving a socially effective persona, who, not having been born with any natural qualifications for instant acceptance in high social circles (name, money, title, beauty, talent), must work at developing assets that are considered desirable by such people.

Although these cultivated credentials provided entrée into high society, they did not qualify her to reach for top-drawer marital material. The men she married were socially acceptable but carried no cachet of family, fortune or title. Worse, they were flawed with weaknesses of character that became manifest in each case after the marriage. Her first husband was a naval lieutenant, Earl Winfield Spencer, Jr., the dashing son of a British mother and a well-to-do American father. Described by his friends as "popular," "a merry devil," and "a good comrade," he seemed the personification of the romantic charmer. But Wallis found, after their lavish wedding, that she had married a foolish, violent drunkard.

Her second husband was Ernest Aldrich Simpson, son of an American mother and a wealthy English father, who was the head of Simpson, Spence and Young, ship brokers with offices in London and New York. Ernest was born and brought up in New York and attended Harvard. In 1918 he went to England and became a second lieutenant in the famed Coldstream Guards and from that point on, his poseur side emerged. Like so many Anglophiles, he became the caricature of the veddy, veddy proper English gentleman complete with guardsman's moustache, bowler and furled umbrella. Though he chose his father's nationality, he did not care to share his religion. According to the *American Examiner-Jewish Week*, Ernest Simpson's family name was Solomon.[10] His son, Henry, born to him and the wife who succeeded Wallis, moved to Israel, and changed his name to Aaron Solomon.[11]

Ernest and Wallis had much in common. They both had one failed marriage, both liked high-style living and both were avid arrivistes. Now solidly situated in his father's vast international company, Ernest was well able to afford to pursue their social ambitions. Immediately after their marriage, they moved into a luxury flat in a fashionable part of London and embarked upon what was destined to become a highly successful career in social climbing. Wallis was a superb cook and hostess due to her early training in Baltimore, and their home soon became a cynosure for a coterie of the upper class and an assortment of interesting people.

After their initial meeting (which took place while Wallis was still married), the charmed prince began dropping in on the Simpsons and soon became a fixture in their home, which made Ernest so proud that he ignored the growing relationship between the prince and Wallis. Instead of being jealous or angry at the attention the prince was publicly lavishing on Wally, social climber Ernest reveled in the honor of being married to the woman coveted by the Prince of Wales and later probably felt honored by being cuckolded by the King of England. According to biographers of the Windsors, "As Wallis's affair with the prince progressed, Simpson's worry was over losing the royal connection—the attitude of a boor, and a *feeble* boor."[12]

For the prince, the Simpsons' flat became the home he always longed for. Wallis played the role of critical parent with which he was familiar but added the affectionate attentiveness he craved. All his affairs had been with married women; he seemed to be drawn to other men's wives and in each case became involved in a family situation, like a small child pressing his nose against the window looking longingly in. It was no secret to his previous lovers that he enjoyed being dominated. Freda Dudley Ward, the woman whom Wally displaced, understood his needs clearly: "I could have dominated him if I had wanted to. I could have done anything with him. Love bewitched him. He made himself the slave of whomever he loved and became totally dependent on her. . . . He liked being humbled, degraded. He BEGGED for it!"[13]

Why, if everyone knew this princely psychological flaw,

could no one else exploit it as effectively as Wallis Simpson? The previous inamoratas were frivolous, beautiful women who were used to playing with men only at the most superficial social level and had no need to develop skills of experience in manipulating psyches. But for Wallis the need to dominate was innate, and not being gifted with the kind of natural beauty that captured men instantly, she had honed instincts and techniques for acquiring control. True, other women recognized the prince's need to be led, but none before Wallis really understood how far one could go in catering to this weakness and how this knowledge could be used to capture the prey. Her predecessors were awed by his royalty, but only Wallis knew that although public chastisement of a prince might look like shocking lèse-majesté, it was mother's milk to him, as evidenced in this famous episode: "The prince, whose table manners were Tudoresque, picked up a scrap of lettuce in his fingers, and Wallis slapped his hand lightly, as would a governess reproving a child."[14] The other guests were horrified at what they regarded as a dreadful gaffe, but the prince obviously ate it up.

There is no doubt that Wallis had made a study of her man and prepared herself accordingly. When the prince began showing interest, she started to read all four leading London newspapers every day from cover to cover so that she could discuss matters of importance with him intelligently. The effectiveness of her ploy was proven by his obvious enchantment with her interest in his daily activities: "She was curious to learn just what a prince's working day consisted of," he recalled of their early days. "She pressed me with questions —hard questions, the questions of a woman who had read a lot and knew something about the new forces at work in the world. . . . Her interest was genuine, and her outlook was new to me. It was a wonderful mixture of warmth, curiosity and independence of spirit, with a wonderful trace of impudence. Right then I made an important discovery; that a man's relationship with a woman could also be an intellectual partnership. That was the start of my falling in love with her. She promised to bring into my life something that wasn't there. I was convinced that with her, I'd be a more creative and useful person."[15]

What a misguided prediction; this was the woman who drove him into a life of total uselessness. That she was able to convince him of the power with which she could surely imbue him was a tribute to her skillful manipulation.

Once he became king of England, the prince decided he must marry Wally because she had become the single most important and controlling force in his life. That he could think for a moment that the nation, the royal family and the government of Great Britain in 1936 would accept a twice-divorced American to be their queen was an indication of his blind adoration and utter obtuseness. The uproar was incredible, and the king's misunderstanding of the public's attitude and total lack of comprehension of the political tides that swirled about him doomed his reign. Wallis, who by this time had him totally under her thumb and to whom he looked for every decision, was shrewd but not smart. The narrow single-mindedness that enabled her to make rapid judgments rendered her blind to needs other than her own, including the king's, whose fate was now hers. Smugly secure that she was indeed the power behind the throne, she suggested a simplistic approach to sway the British people: just talk to them on the radio, as President Roosevelt did with his fireside chats. Tell them our story, and they're bound to come over to your side. That sort of direct emotional appeal may have been effective many years later on American television with Richard Nixon, but unfortunately Edward VIII did not have a dog named Checkers and a wife with a plain Republican cloth coat. In the 1930s the English were not ready to accept Wallis as their queen. Not only were they angry at the infamous Mrs. Simpson, but there was fury directed at a king who would put this tarnished woman above his duty to the nation. Even the idea of a public relations gambit such as a national address showed Wally's and the king's abysmal ignorance of British law: before a monarch could go before the commonwealth with a political issue, consent of the government was required. Stanley Baldwin, as prime minister, was violently opposed to the liaison, and turned down the request.

And so, 326 days after his coronation, King Edward VIII abdicated his throne "for the woman I love" in one of the most memorable broadcasts in the history of radio. It was a historic event and the entire English-speaking world stopped to listen. Imagine, the king of England giving up his throne for a woman . . . not a great beauty, not a great charmer, not a great anything! What has SHE got that captivated and mesmerized a monarch?

Wallis Warfield Simpson offered the prince everything his feared/revered papa gave him, plus the affection he withheld. She disparaged yet "darlinged" him. She treated him with the disdain he felt he deserved, yet showed him the love he craved. It was the combination he had been seeking all his life.

In the pathetic, aimless afterlife of the Duke of Windsor, Wally enabled him finally to realize his and his father's expectations—colossal failure. It was a role in which he was totally comfortable. Until the end of his life, Wallis demeaned him publicly and privately. She never ceased to blame him for the abdication, indicating that a wiser, more able man could have handled it better, so that he could have remained on the throne and eventually made her his queen. She never forgave him for failing to secure for her the proper title, something that gnawed at both of them forever and for which she constantly baited him. In the worldly scheme of things, and considering the nation-shattering event they effected, one would think that proper mode of address would have been of minor importance to the Duchess. But to a couple such as the Windsors, whose entire lives were spent in the pursuit of petty pleasures, such an affront loomed large. She could only be addressed as "Your Grace" and referred to as "Her Grace" and never, as befitting the wife of a prince, "her royal highness." But so deep was the bitterness toward this woman whom the royal family viewed as an adventuress that the Duke's brother, now king, refused to allow her the title. It was a slap at Wally that rankled all of her life, and she never let her poor husband forget it. Forever, she faulted him for his obvious ineptitude in being unable to obtain the respect that was her due, and she punished him daily for his weaknesses.

"An exchange overheard in Neuilly" went something like this:

DUCHESS:	'David, come here a moment.'
DUKE:	'Just a second, darling, I have something on my mind.'
DUCHESS:	'On your *what*?'
DUKE:	(apologetically) 'I know, darling. I haven't much of a mind.' "[16]

There were times when her open contempt drove him to actual tears. It was a sad culmination to the love affair of the century, yet his adoration for her never faltered. What did Wallis Simpson have that made her the obsession of a king? She had the qualities he admired in his father: strength and utter self-assurance and a sharp, reproving tongue. In his book, he says, "I admired her forthrightness. If she disagreed with some point under discussion, she never failed to advance her own views with vigor and spirit. That side of her enchanted me."[17]

She presented the image of independence, the free, indomitable spirit that he longed to be: "In character, Wallis was, and still remains, complex and elusive; and from the first I looked upon her as the most independent woman I had ever met."[18]

She conveyed to him the sense of being unattainable:

"And then one day she began to mean more to me in a way that she did not perhaps comprehend. My impression is that for a long time she remained unaffected by my interest."[19]

I'll bet.

She directed, dominated and disparaged him so that he could actually be the ineffectual dolt his father had trained him to be and thus fulfill his predestination.

How much of Wally's behavior was natural and how much affected is impossible to compute, but I would say that it was a combination of both. She was the perfect person to psych the damaged psyche of a pathetic prince; she instinctively recognized his weaknesses and needs and how they could be reached by her strengths. She succeeded beyond even her wildest dreams.

It has often been said that men marry their mothers. The Prince of Wales, King Edward VIII, Duke of Windsor married his father.

References

1. J. Bryan III and Charles J. V. Murphy, *The Windsor Story*, New York: William Morrow and Company, Inc., 1979, p. 367.
2. H. R. H. Edward, Duke of Windsor, *A King's Story: The Memoirs of the Duke of Windsor*, New York: G. P. Putnam's Sons, 1947, 1950, 1951, p. 28. With the courtesy of the Institut Pasteur.
3. Treat Gabriel, *Call of the Wildmen*, New York *Times Magazine*, October 14, 1990, p. 42.
4. *Ibid.*, p. 28.
5. *Ibid.*, p. 58.
6. *Ibid.*, p. 104.
7. *Ibid.*, p. 257.

8. Bryan and Murphy, *op. cit.*, p. 20.

9. *Ibid.*, p. 20.

10. *Ibid.*, p. 45.

11. *Ibid.*, p. 483.

12. *Ibid.*, p. 53.

13. *Ibid.*, p. 98.

14. *Ibid.*, p. 97.

15. Windsor, *op. cit.*, p. 93.

16. *Ibid.*, p. 555.

17. Windsor, *op. cit.*, p. 258.

18. *Ibid.*, p. 258.

19. *Ibid.*, p. 258.

CHAPTER XII

OTHER WEDDED
WINNERS

WHEN YOU MEET PEOPLE at a party who haven't seen you for a while, their usual question is, "How've you been?" When you're a writer, the question becomes, "So what are you working on?" With my past five books, I'd name the title, heads would nod and the conversation would go on to more interesting matters.

Not so with this book. As soon as the title was out of my mouth, all heads within listening radius would snap up and within minutes I was surrounded by interested kibitzers. Everybody had a suggestion. Everybody had an opinion. Suddenly, everyone was an expert on who would be the ideal candidate for this book, or was ready to challenge my choices.

"Who the hell is Alma Mahler?" (That inevitably from the forty-and-under crowd. The fifty-and-over bunch usually recognized the name at once and many of them would start singing Tom Lehrer's lyrics.)

"Michelle Marvin? Who's she?" (All I had to do was mention "palimony" and the light of comprehension would shine forth.)

Ultimately I evolved my own little "recognition analysis" game to see if I could predict an individual's reaction to the names of women included in the book based on what I perceived as his or her interests and background. For instance, I learned to expect cultured people to recognize the name of Françoise Gilot at once. People who kept up with the *New York Times Book Review* knew Slim Keith, as her book, *Slim*, had been on the bestseller list for a number of weeks within the past year.

The biggest annoyance was the people who attacked me for not including their favorite multiple-marriers, shaking their heads sadly as though I had made a fatal error. As I tired of pointing out, a woman who married many men in the same field or profession is not unusual because it stands to reason that those are the circles in which she traveled and in which she would meet the same kind of men. There's no question about "What has *she* got?" She just has entrée to and familiarity with a specific group of men.

The most frequently suggested name was Jackie Kennedy Onassis. But she doesn't qualify at all. At the time of her marriage to the brash and profligate young second-generation Irish son of a bootlegger, she was an elegant beauty from a society family. Only the fact that he had reached the elevated position of senator, through Lord knows what kind of improper Bostonian political chicanery, qualified him to be Jacqueline Bouvier's husband. In fact, in many circles it was considered that she had married beneath her. Her second marriage to Aristotle Onassis was strictly a business deal. The only reason Ari wanted Jackie was because she was the widow of the slain president of the United States and the most famous, most emulated style-setter in the world—for him, a real coup. Onassis was continually in ferocious competition with his brother-in-law, Stavros Niarchos, each one trying to outdo the other in acquisitions. Jackie Kennedy was the most prestigious acquisition of the era—now let's see Stavros top THIS.

There were a number of other women who qualified, but because limitations of space and time did not make it. Here are a few of the runners-up:

ALANA HAMILTON STEWART
The Woman Who Won George Hamilton and Rod Stewart

How does a willowy blonde from a dirt-poor family in Nacogdoches, Texas, end up with $25,000 a month in alimony from one of the major rock stars of the day?

Alana Collins was a stunning twenty-two-year-old Ford model when she started dating the actor George Hamilton, whose claims to fame were a perpetual tan and his page-one romance with President Lyndon Johnson's daughter Lynda Bird. George and Alana had two things in common: both came from small towns (Hamilton was born in Blytheville, Arkansas) and both had mothers who had been married four times, but they came from different sides of the tracks.

After living together on and off for four years, to everyone's shock they got married. George is a very classy guy who is very conscious of social standing. Under the tutelage of his mother, the overriding influence in his life, he has developed a unique-to-Hollywood style of moving freely and easily among the elite of the social, international and show-biz worlds and managing through shrewdly invisible financial deals to support his elegant life-style. He is known to be a clever real estate investor who buys and sells properties at hefty profits. He has been reputed to do well in the stock market and in the late seventies and eighties hung around with Saul Steinberg and that winning circle of tycoons who were making millions. He was also involved in personally profitable financial deals with Imelda Marcos. He went out with the likes of Charlotte Ford, Wendy Vanderbilt, Vanessa Redgrave, Jeanne Moreau and Candice Bergen. Through his mother's old friend, the New York socialite Cobina Wright, he met Merle Oberon, who took him on as a pet; he became part of the important Old Hollywood set, which included Louis B. Mayer's daughter Edie Goetz.

George cut a wide swath in Tinseltown without ever having achieved stardom. He was a guest in the grandest houses in Hollywood and then moved on to the most famous house of them all, the White House. He was introduced to Lynda Bird by Charlotte Ford, and they had their first date at a dinner for Princess Margaret and Lord Snowden.

Lynda Bird Johnson and Alana Collins are both from Texas. But what made him marry Alana? They ran off to Las Vegas on October 29, 1972, and were married in jeans with Colonel Tom Parker, Elvis's manager, as their sole witness. He claims it was a spur-of-the-moment decision, but nothing in George Hamilton's past indicates that he does anything without careful consideration.

George was then thirty-three, too old to be still unmarried by Southern standards. Southerners believe in matrimony as an important part of life, which is why they do it so often. Their concept of the nuptial vows differs somewhat from the rest of the country's, as witness the many cheatin' songs so popular in Country-Western music, but they do believe in marrying over and over again. By the age of thirty-three, George's mother had already had a passel of husbands, and it is more than likely that George felt his time had come. As he put it in an article in the January 1991 issue of *Vanity Fair*, "I wanted to get married and settle down." Alana was already living in his house, she was an accepted member of the filmdom celebrity circle, she was beautiful, and her background hearkened back to the real George Hamilton.

Although his mother, Anne Hamilton, now eighty and living in a posh oceanfront condominium in Palm Beach, brought her sons up in upper-crust style, they never had real money and scrounged along, part of the small legion of pseudosocialite aspirants who mingle with and take on the lifestyles of the wealthy but continually struggle to afford the tariff. George was born and lived until the age of seven in a small Arkansas town, where his uncle owned the hardware store and his grandfather was the doctor. Deep down, that's where the real George Hamilton was formed, that's the part of him that felt kindred to Alana Collins. In the same *Vanity Fair* article, he mentions that his visit to Alana's hometown brought back happy memories of his childhood, and as he put it, "I saw there was a reality about Alana."

But marriage to Alana did not turn out to be the settled domesticity George had expected. They had a son, Ashley, (named after the *Gone with the Wind* character played by Leslie Howard), who is now sixteen years old and six feet four inches, but they broke up after five years and divorced in 1977. When asked the reason for the split, George claimed their differences were based on Alana's love of flashy Hollywood partying and his weariness of the whole scene.

According to *Cosmopolitan*'s April 1988 article "The Single Girls of Beverly Hills," Alana was still at it after her divorce from millionaire rock singer Rod Stewart: "She's a star of Hollywood's party circuit . . . she's a good friend, good sport, great flirt. Watching her handle a chance meeting with Sylvester Stallone at a party is like watching Madame de Pompadour in her prime. Long blonde hair, lithe tennis player's body and a laugh that goes on into the wee hours is how to identify Alana Stewart." Let's not forget that at the time of the article she was forty-two years old, but then, as Gloria Steinem once said to an admirer who told her when her birthday arrived that she didn't look forty, "This is what forty looks like." Looking at Alana and Candice and Gloria and Farrah, you are reassured that sex appeal defies the calendar.

Alana married Rod Stewart in 1979, and their divorce came through in December 1990, although they have been legally apart since 1984. Alana now lives with her three children (she has a ten-year-old and an eleven-year-old with Rod Stewart and Ashley moves between her and his father) in splendor so elegant it has earned her the media title "The Baroness of Brentwood."

After reading George Hamilton's version of the reason for their divorce, I felt Alana deserved equal time.

"Our marriage broke up because I was in a different place then," she told me. "I was younger . . . people go in different directions. I wanted different things then than I want now.

"I liked being married. Now I'd like to have a really happy, functional relationship and success in the work I'm doing. My priorities now are my children and my work. I want to be successful now in my own right."

When I asked what her new work is, she told me she is now writing the third of three screenplays, and Warner Brothers is producing one of them. I was very impressed that someone who has no background or training in writing could produce salable material in the dog-eat-dog world of TV and films, until she mentioned that she is working with a collaborator, Carole Bayer Sager. Now that's the advantage of living in baronial splendor on an income of about half a million a year and being the ex-wife of big stars—you get to meet people such as Carole Sager and are even allowed to collaborate with them. Producers are always conscious of the star-pull of names on their projects. The skillful writing of a Carole Sager together with the glitzy name of Alana Stewart is bound to pull 'em in at the box office.

Alana told me that she wants to change her image; she no longer wants to be known as a woman who married famous men. "I'm in a different place now," she says. She sure is— there's nothing like starting at the top when you embark upon a second career. But if your first career was marrying well, the next one is bound to be a piece of cake.

PHYLLIS CERF
Wife of Two of New York's Finest

Phyllis Cerf was the wife of Bennett Cerf, the urbane bon vivant publisher and one of the bright-boy literati who founded Random House. He became a major TV personality who appeared regularly on popular shows such as *What's My Line?* and Phyllis and Bennett were part of the highly visible intellectual and social elite of New York. After he died, Phyllis was a rather dumpy middle-aged widow who could never keep up with the stylish slimness of her friends. Yet, within a few years, she married New York City's most eligible bachelor, Robert Wagner, Jr., the former mayor and son of highly respected Senator Robert Wagner. From the moment Bob Wagner's wife, Susan, died, he became the target of ambitious women everywhere: he was a prime catch. The newspapers chronicled his social life and dates with beautiful models, women twenty years his junior, famous women, achieving women, all seeking the cachet of an alliance with so prominent a man. Yet he chose to marry chunky Phyllis. And all the women who tried and lost look at her and wonder, "Now what has *she* got?"

Then there are the women who married only once, but the groom was so stellar and the bride so ordinary that one does wonder, "What has *she* got?"

LINDA McCARTNEY
The Beatle Snatcher

Millions of young women were fainting at his feet. Girls all over the world were drooling at his picture. He could have had virtually any woman in the world, and he chose to marry a nice Jewish girl from Scarsdale. She's pretty, but not stunning, she's intelligent but not brilliant, she's pleasant but not sparkling. True, she was a working photographer, but Linda Eastman was hardly in the Scavullo-Avedon-Adams class. How did she capture the sought-after attention and love of Paul McCartney?

Most likely it was just that calm, cool ordinariness that attracted a man who was constantly exposed to hysterical, aggressive gorgeous girls and women. To a man weary of being pursued and torn at, she conveyed elusiveness and unattainability.

"I twisted Linda's arm and she agreed to marry me," he told *US* magazine in the February 1990 issue. You got that? HE had to convince HER. "Linda was afraid it wouldn't work out and I kept telling her, 'Aw, come on, it will be fine. Don't worry,' And I'm still telling her that."

As Françoise Gilot said, when you want them, they don't want you. Linda Eastman projected an unconcern with his fame that was unusual for him to encounter and a lack of interest he found provocative. It's an attitude she apparently still maintains so that he is continually titillated with uncertainty. It's the kind of independent pose that Michelle Marvin assumes with Dick Van Dyke that keeps him off balance with the anticipation that she might take off at any moment.

Linda conveys a feeling of passivity, but underneath there is a core of strength, which is apparent from McCartney's further statements: "She's very ballsy, Linda. She's not the kind of person people think she is at all. Her image is very different from how she is."

The calm exterior masks the I-can-take-your-crap-but-I'll-get-what-I-want-anyway interior developed by women, such as Françoise Gilot, who have domineering fathers and who have developed their own brand of survival tactics. Linda Eastman's father is an attorney known for being tough, who has successfully represented most of the leading abstract expressionist artists in the country, and who, together with Linda's brother, manages some of McCartney's millions.

That seems to be a pattern with the Beatles—Yoko Ono's financier family handled John Lennon's fortune also, and probably still does.

QUEEN FABIOLA OF BELGIUM,
The Plain Lady Who Became Queen

Fabiola de Mora y Aragon was a colorless, thirtyish Spanish woman from an aristocratic family when she met Prince Royal Baudouin of Belgium. The eldest son of the controversial King Leopold III, he was destined to inherit the throne eventually, but assumed it prematurely when his father was forced to abdicate.

Leopold III had been a popular monarch at first, but when he surrendered the Belgian army to the Germans after a gallant resistance during World War II, the people turned against him. When the war ended, many Belgians refused to have him as their ruler. His son was given the role of regent until he reached the age of twenty-one, at which time he ascended the throne.

Young, blonde, handsome, the young prince was the most eligible royal catch of the time. He was pursued by international beauties, heiresses, glamorous actresses and nymphets; every European royal family with a marriageable daughter arranged meetings and panted in anticipation. Everyone wanted a shot at this title. When he became king in 1951, the pursuit became frenetic. Here was a man with a real throne, a palace to live in and a nation of subjects paying him homage.

As the king approached the age of thirty, which was old for an unmarried monarch, and even more princesses were reaching marriageable age, international nobility was becoming desperate. What in heaven and earth is he looking for? Imagine their shock when he announced his engagement in 1960, not to some royal beauty or even to some knockout movie star such as Grace Kelly, but to an undistinguished, ordinary Spanish woman of whom no one had ever heard. Journalists all over the world scrambled to check up on her background. Who was she? Where did she come from? All they learned was that she was royally acceptable, however low the level, because she came from an aristocratic family. But, horror of horrors, she was over thirty! They had a name for women like that back in those days: they were spoken of with pity as spinsters. And to top off the ignominy felt by all the rejected candidates, she was actually older than he. To all the diligent royalty matchmakers throughout Europe who had lost their prime candidate, the whole matter was incredible and incomprehensible.

Suddenly the shy, dark-haired Fabiola was on front pages all over the world, and women everywhere looked at her picture wonderingly and asked, "What has she got?"

To this day, the question remains unanswered. In the ensuing years, nothing about the queen has emerged to indicate that she is, in fact, anything more than ordinary. Why did Baudouin pick her? Maybe ordinary is all he wanted because that's just what he is, a very ordinary man thrust into an extraordinary position.

He may have been overwhelmed by other women's glamour, beauty and achievement; those kinds of people may be nice to visit, but hell to live with. The teenage bimbo princesses may be delightful to look at, but what do you talk about? Fabiola and he share the same eras and have similar frames of reference. This nice quiet woman makes him feel happy and comfortable and makes his palace a home. What more could any king want? Looking at the latest photographs of an alternately morose and disgruntled Prince Charles, one wonders if he doesn't sometimes wish he had made a similar choice.

CHAPTER XIII

THE CONFLICT BETWEEN
FEMINISM AND
FEMME-FATALISM

THE WOMEN IN THIS BOOK have chosen derivative desti-
nies. They have refined the age-old behavior of male-pleasing to a high art and have succeeded possibly beyond their
dreams. Before the advent of feminism, we were all forced
to follow that route. But now, we scorn such sublimation
because we can achieve success on our own and no longer
have to do it as clingers to the coattails of men.

My tendency, and perhaps the tendency of all women today whose consciousness has been raised to the awareness
that we have won the right to realize ourselves as individuals
in many arenas, is to look upon these women with some
contempt. But am I, and are you, if you share this feeling,
being totally fair? The goal of the women's movement is to
offer the option of choice and to allow women to select their
own routes to fulfillment, whether it be at home, in the mar-
ketplace or in the professions. A woman now can evaluate
her abilities and needs and dreams and make her own decision concerning how she will spend her life.

For the women described in this book, was it demeaning
to subordinate self in order to achieve reflected fame or was
it worthwhile? After all, we are told that it is practical to

215

become reconciled to our limitations and to use whatever means we have available to achieve personal aims. If they, and other women out there, have goals that do not match up with their abilities, if nature unfortunately did not endow them with the original equipment required to reach the fame they long for, is it not sensible to use whatever qualities they have in order to get it, or at least to get as close as possible?

If devoting themselves to catering to outstanding men enables them to reach the aura of fame rather than the actuality, then we must regard it as a wise compromise. Actually, how different is their calculated male-servility from the people-pandering practiced by ambitious men and women in business and the professions in order to reach their goals? Talent agents are subservient grovelers to their clients in order to get derivative income and fame. And how about the young junior executives who regard sucking up to the boss as mandatory behavior in order to move up the corporate ladder? It's a fact of life that everything's a trade-off, and each person must decide what she is willing to give up in order to get what she wants.

Little girls often have fantasies of being rich and famous, but most reconcile to reality during the growing-up years. The women portrayed in this book never did. Their dreams developed into obsessions that drove them to such self-deception that giving away pieces of themselves was viewed as but a casual casualty; transmogrification was acceptable as long as it achieved the desired effect.

If you are looking for congruity among these women, and an answer to the question "What has SHE got?", it is the hunger to achieve highly visible public acknowledgment of being head-and-shoulders above other women, plus the ability to be self-delusionary about the degree of significant self-sacrifice demanded to achieve that goal.

You, I, any of us could do it. All you have to do is decide, would it be worth it?

INDEX

217